THE **COMPLETE GUIDE** TO

TRAINING WITH FREE WEIGHTS

Dedicated to my father, who I admire and respect more than anyone else and to my late mother who always believed in and inspired me.

THE COMPLETE GUIDE TO

Graeme Marsh

TRAINING WITH FREE WEIGHTS

A & C Black • London

First published 2008
A&C Black Publishers Ltd
38 Soho Square
London
W1D 3HB
www.acblack.com

Copyright © 2008 Graeme Marsh

ISBN 9780713685466

A CIP catalogue record for this book is available from the British Library.

Cover and all inside photographs © Grant Pritchard
Contrast training set on page 120 © Chris Thibaudeau, reproduced by kind permission

This book is produced using paper that is made from wood grown in managed, sustainable forests. It is natural, renewable and recyclable. The logging and manufacturing processes conform to the environmental regulations of the country of origin.

Typeset in Baskerville by Palimpsest Book Production Ltd, Grangemouth, Stirlingshire

Manufactured by South China Printing Company, Ltd., China

CONTENTS

ACKNOWLEDGEMENTS

As ever there is a long list of people whose help and guidance have made this project possible to complete and this is my best opportunity to say thank you for all their support. Principal thanks go to my ever faithful and patient business partner Greg Smith, who keeps the ship afloat while I am away, and to my father – Anthony Marsh – who has been an invaluable sounding board, advisor, and source of help throughout. Thanks also to my close friends and colleagues, who have been constantly supportive and understanding of the challenges involved in completing this project alongside everything else.

A huge thank you is in order for my ever-patient editors at A&C Black and a large thank you goes out to all my clients, both past and present, who I work with regularly and greatly enjoy spending my time with.

To all of the team at Aegis Training in London, where fitness really is an overriding passion and an inspiration to us all to keep working on improving and developing our skills.

A big thank you to the models: Dave Fletcher – www.dfpt.co.uk; Elaine Tilley – elaine@ corrective-exercise.co.uk; Stephen Aish – steve@londonkettlebells.com; Mike Causer – causer-michael@hotmail.com; and Nicola Rennie.

Finally, thanks go to all those who have helped develop my skills and improve my knowledge and to all my colleagues and friends in the fitness, media and personal training industry in the UK and USA. In particular, those strength coaches and exercise experts who have helped develop my skills and knowledge and who have influenced me this far, and many, many others who have had a part in my life and career so far, I am very grateful to you all.

Graeme

PART **ONE**

GETTING STARTED

Training with free weights isn't as simple as just walking into the gym, picking up a barbell and going for it. Lifting weights safely and effectively needs guidance, tuition, not to mention a bit of nerve to brave the sometimes intimidating and alien atmosphere of a busy weights room.

A commercial opportunity was spotted in the 1970s, a way to get ordinary people resistance training without any instruction or challenge and before very long health clubs everywhere were packed with shiny (and very expensive) ranges of machines. These removed the need for lifting weights with a barbell or dumbbells by working individual muscle groups in isolation, often in the form of a circuit.

While the machines promised fantastic results, ease of use for all, and access to the previously forbidden world of strength training, in many ways they sold the public short. While this book is not totally against the use of any method of exercise at any given time, there are a few reasons why I am such a strong advocate of free weights over machines and these are shown below.

- **Is a machine any safer than a free weight?** This is probably the most common reason why people choose to use a machine rather than a free weight, usually because they can sit at a machine, machines have a fixed plane of movement, and they require less skill to use. The truth is that it is just as easy to hurt yourself on a machine as it is with a weight. Many machines actually place the user in their weakest position to start the exercise, placing stress on the joint structures. Worse still, the ease with which people can use them often leads to poor (frequently dangerous) technique and form. Remember, any exercise done badly is likely to be harmful, whether on a machine or not.

- **They both work the same muscles, so what's the difference?** When it comes to working the whole body, fixed resistance machines fall a long way behind a good free weight movement. Most machines work individual muscle groups in isolation rather than together with the other muscles that they normally operate with, which means that you would have to use many different ones to recreate the kind of muscle activation that is seen from an exercise such as a clean and press or a deadlift. This stabilised and fixed environment also removes the need for the other muscles in the body to provide the stability that is essential in everyday life, further reducing the demand on the body for energy and coordination.

- **I'm a beginner, so isn't a machine easier for me to start on?** Using fixed machines removes the need for the body to provide the stability that is essential in movement. By taking away this demand our development in essential areas such as balance, coordination, bodily awareness, and others is limited. When we begin weight training, the major adaptations come in the nervous system rather than in the physical structure of the muscle. Starting out is a time when we should aim to *increase* the stability demands of an exercise for maximum results, not decrease it.

- **I'm worried about my joints, are free weights safe?** Many machines allow the user to compromise joint safety through poor technique to overcome the selected resistance. By isolating joints we often *increase* the forces going through that joint, placing it at a higher risk of damage. An example of this is the leg extension machine, common in most health clubs. Compared to the free weight exercise of a squat, the leg extension exercise works less muscle and generates large amounts of joint forces without the assistance of other muscles around the knee to provide stability. This couldn't be further from the way these muscles work in real life and does very little to protect the joint. As if that wasn't reason enough, many machines have a fixed pattern of movement that is not always achievable by all users, forcing them to work in an uncomfortable and potentially injurious position.

There are many other false truths that circulate about machine training. Though there is a place for the use of some machines, such as in very early stage rehabilitation, they should not form the main focus of a resistance training programme. The key to remember with most machines is that they are designed to train muscles not movement.

Weight training and other disciplines

Free weights can form an excellent supplementary training programme for a wide range of sports and activities. They are used extensively by athletes in sports ranging from sprinting to rugby to help improve performance, reduce injury, speed recovery, and overcome training plateaux such as the development of explosive power in football or to increase bodyweight in contact sports.

However, there are still people who make erroneous claims about weight training to better promote their own choice of activity. One of these claims is that doing weights will make muscles bulky and inflexible and that activities such as Pilates, in fact, lengthen muscles creating a long and lean physique. While this might be an appealing notion to some, it is in fact a long way from the truth about how our muscles function and respond to training.

The fact is that *any* muscle action involves contracting muscles; we can't move without a muscle contracting, even stretching a muscle involves contracting another. These relationships are how joints stay in one place. If every muscle were long and loose then we'd end up with slack muscles everywhere and we wouldn't be able to move at all! These claims also show an ignorance of the wide range of exercises and outcomes that a well-designed weight training programme can provide, choosing instead to focus on an outdated stereotypical idea of the overdeveloped and inflexible individual that is far from the reality.

All for weights, and weights for all!

There is a strong case for free weight training to form some part of just about everybody's life. The profound range of benefits it offers can appeal to everyone, from children to grandparents, men and women alike.

Through improvements in research, programme design, and equipment availability we are all able to achieve our goals with the use of free weights, either on their own or as part of a balanced exercise programme.

Weight training need not mean being excessively bulky, inflexible, or unhealthy. In fact, weight training can frequently offer a greater variety of exercises and benefits such as core stability, better posture and flexibility, improved body composition, and all-round better health, compared to many other methods of exercise.

The key to success with weight training is the correct selection of exercises and acute exercise variables (such as sets, reps, tempo, rest period, and load) to achieve your goals. By developing a simple understanding of these you can design your own training programme to start lifting weights safely and effectively.

Human movement and function

Many books on exercise and fitness have exhaustive sections on the anatomy and physiology of how muscles function at a microscopic level and sometimes you can miss the bigger picture. Understanding how we function on a global level is actually far more important to all but the most hardened of sports scientists. Over time the study of sciences such as biomechanics, kinesiology, and physiology have given us some substantial insights into the way that the human body moves and functions. Yet as our understanding of the importance of movement increases, everyday life is working against us to make us less active than ever. More and more people now spend their days in front of a computer screen, while kids are also less active physically. Although we might be living longer, musculoskeletal health is getting worse, while the growing obesity epidemic could have grave consequences for the health of the nation.

Despite all this knowledge, though, many people perform programmes of exercise that don't reflect the movements they would like to improve and frequently neglect areas such as

balance, stability, agility, and the multi-directional nature of everyday life and sport.

Muscles in action

Although Newton may not have been considering the human body when he came up with one of his most well known truisms – every action has an equal and opposite reaction – he had perfectly described how the muscular system of the body works to give us the ability to move and function with relative ease.

For us to move a weight or resistance we need some muscles to shorten (concentric action), others we need to lengthen (eccentric or opposite action), while yet others need to create a force to stabilise the body against the forces we are generating (isometric or equal action). To make this a bit clearer, let's consider one of the most well known exercises, the press-up.

Ask just about anybody what the press-up exercise focuses on and they'll tell you it's a great movement for strengthening the chest, and they would be right. But a closer look at the press-up actually tells us that there is a lot more than just the chest having to do some work here.

As we lower into the press-up, the muscles across the front of the shoulder have to lengthen (eccentric action) along with those on the back of the arms. This lengthening controls our descent towards the floor as we resist the urge of gravity to smack us face first into the earth. As we do this though, a whole host of other muscles are hard at work to keep the body in the press-up position. All around the shoulder and hip in particular, smaller postural muscles function as stabilisers to keep joints functioning at their optimal position (isometric actions). In particular, during the press-up, the abdominals must work to keep the body in good alignment from head to toe. Without these muscles functioning, there would be no stable platform for the muscles of the chest, shoulders, and arms to propel us back up into the start position (concentric action). If the stabilising muscles of the body stop functioning correctly, it can lead to real problems, and these muscles should not be neglected in any training programme.

Without these equal and opposite actions that our muscles perform, we simply wouldn't be able to move or function. However, many modern training approaches seem to have forgotten this and become focused on training individual muscles as if they were independent from the rest of the body. When we do this it can lead to imbalances developing and problems with posture and pain.

Every exercise, even the most simple, is a skilled movement that needs many muscles to coordinate together to perform. Strengthening of the entire movement should be the aim, rather than the strength of a single muscle or joint action. Unless your sole focus is hypertrophy for bodybuilding, stop thinking about individual muscles and start thinking movement. The application of bodybuilding techniques for most people is outdated and much training doctrine has been greatly influenced by the use of anabolic substances and should not be applied without good consideration.

The importance of eccentric muscle action in weight training

All too often when people begin training with free weights they concentrate their attention on the lifting portion of the exercise and give scant time to the lowering (eccentric) part of the movement. However, research has proven that the lowering phase of a movement is highly valuable to strength development.

For many years, serious strength trainers and bodybuilders have used eccentric (also known as negative rep) training to stimulate greater strength gains and muscle growth. Beware, though, of too much heavy eccentric style training, as it leads to prolonged muscle soreness and overtraining due to the stress it places on the body.

The eccentric phase of a movement also places a stretch on the muscle that can provide us with greater impetus for the concentric phase of a movement. A simple example of this is the countermovement we would use if someone asked us to jump as high as we possibly could. By dropping down first we stretch and load muscles before they explosively shorten and propel us upwards.

This type of training has become known as plyometrics and is widely accepted as a method for developing speed strength or power.

Fundamental movement patterns – training movements over muscles

For many years when it came to weight training, exercises were assigned pride of place in a workout based on which major muscles they targeted. Training routines would often focus on hitting the chest and triceps or quads and shoulders. The theory was that a muscle got such an intense amount of work during the session that it would not need working for another week.

This type of training is known as a split routine and is covered in later chapters. Although many bodybuilders over the years used this approach with success, there are other approaches that are well suited to training for outcomes other than simple muscle size. Our brain doesn't think in terms of muscles, it thinks in terms of movements. Effective movement comes from coordinating many different muscles (with different functions) to work together.

As resistance training has become more popular, we have started to identify common patterns of movement that can be recreated with free weights exercises. Not only do these movement patterns help to simplify training programme design, they also help in designing balanced programmes of exercise that can help prevent injury from muscle imbalances caused by repeatedly overworking certain muscles.

To help understand how we move and function we will be using the following categories of movement throughout this book alongside the primary muscles involved.

- Squat and lift – knee and hip dominant
- Push/pull – vertical or horizontal
- Lunge and step

Using these movement categories it is possible to design programmes of exercise that are specific to the movements that you want to train. Of course, just as we rarely ever operate in one plane of movement, we also use combinations of different movement patterns to generate an action. Combining different movement patterns can lead to designing exercises that train both muscles and movements in a way that is simply not possible with the use of machines.

Some of the best examples of this can be seen in Olympic-style lifts that although usually performed with a barbell, can also be done with dumbbells, kettlebells, or powerbags. The Olympic lifts, such as cleans and snatches, demand mobility, strength, power, and skill to be performed correctly. These are shown in Chapter 6. Alternatively, movements can be grouped together to form an individual exercise, repetition, or set. This is known as a hybrid, complex, or combination and is covered later (see p. 121).

Muscle fibre types – the tortoise and the hare . . .

Although essentially muscle is muscle, when we look at it a bit closer there are some fairly significant differences to be seen. Broadly speaking, muscle fibres in the body fall into two categories – slow twitch (also known as type 1 or red fibres) and fast twitch (also known as type 2 or white fibres). Although our individual make up of muscle is largely determined by our genes, we can influence it through the way we train, which is important to consider when designing a training programme.

Type 1 or slow twitch fibres – the tortoises

Type 1 muscle fibres activate at low levels, contract slowly, and are highly resistant to fatigue. They also contain high levels of enzymes and cells that promote aerobic activity (where oxygen helps to maintain energy production), which means that they are not built for speed, but rather endurance. They are smaller in size than the type 2 fibres and have key roles in keeping good posture, as well as in endurance sports such as running and cycling. Although type 1 fibres may grow (or hypertrophy) in response to weight training, they don't grow to the extent that type 2 fibres will.

Type 2 or fast twitch fibres – the hares

These are the rapidly contracting but quickly fatiguing fibres. They are powered by energy within the muscle and operate anaerobically (without using oxygen) and are much better suited to high-intensity training and speed work. Truly the hare in comparison to the type 1 fibres, the type 2 fibres can develop force rapidly (about ten times quicker) and in great amounts but not without cost as they quickly tire and run out of steam leaving the tortoise to pick up the slack.

What fibre type are you?

Although the average person may have a 50/50 split of muscle fibres, there are clearly some marked differences between individuals and genders. Women tend to have a greater number of the type 1 fibres than men, for example. In fact, some women's type 1 fibres are actually larger in cross-sectional area than their type 2 fibres – a fact which may help explain why women are unable to generate the same type of power output as men and why they tend to be more resistant to fatigue in high-intensity exercise.

Adaptation, the basis of life, and free-weight training

One of the first and most fundamental principles for understanding how we can develop strength and fitness is the ability to adapt to stress. This process was researched and modelled by Canadian biologist Hans Selye in his 1956 work, *The Stress of Life.* Since then, Selye's model – known as the general adaptation syndrome (GAS) – has been used to explain how the body reacts and adapts to weight training

(both acutely and chronically), which is in itself a form of stress to the body.

Selye identified three stages in how the body reacts to a stressor. These are shown in figure 1.1.

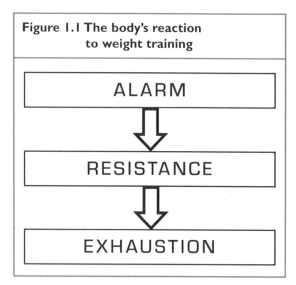

Figure 1.1 The body's reaction to weight training

ALARM

RESISTANCE

EXHAUSTION

Let's look at this model in the context of someone new to weight training. A new exposure to a workout routine (such as when someone lifts weights for the first time) triggers an alarm response. During this response, the body is struggling to cope with the new stress often resulting in soreness and a temporary drop in performance.

As the trainee is repeatedly exposed to the same workout stress, the body starts to respond through changes in the various bodily systems. Although we often think of muscles growing through weight training, the first responses come from the nervous system, which in turn stimulates changes in the other systems of the body (endocrine, musculoskeletal, metabolic, and cardiovascular) that form the human movement system.

However, it is not quite as straightforward as just continually stressing the body and gaining a positive response. The body needs time to adapt and recover from stress and without this it becomes exhausted, potentially leading to a condition known as overtraining.

The old adage that a change is as good as a rest also bears a strong element of truth. If we fail to change the stress on the body and persist with the same workout routine, week in – week out, then the gains that we make begin to quickly drop as our body adapts fully to the stress. It is this principle that has guided the development of periodisation, a method of organising training to prevent overtraining and staleness while improving performance. This is covered in greater detail in Chapter 9.

It is also important to remember that there are other aspects to life beyond the training plan that can contribute to our levels of physiological stress. Lack of sleep, poor nutrition, work, relationships, and other emotional stressors can also have a significant affect on our ability to cope with stress. This is important to remember when designing a programme of exercise – some stress is necessary for positive changes in the body, but too much can lead to exhaustion, lack of progression and overtraining. By managing the stress in our lives and training, we can keep the body moving between alarm and resistance, prompting positive changes and increases in fitness and health.

The four keys to successful training

We have established that the process of adaptation is an essential part of free weight training. The type and extent of this adaptation is governed by the design of a training programme to elicit certain responses from the trainee. To ensure that the training programme is effective at getting the desired results there are four key areas that must be satisfied: specificity, overload, accommodation, and individualisation.

Specificity

The body adapts to training in very specific ways, so if we want a certain outcome from our programme then that must be reflected in the choice of exercises and variables, such as sets, reps, tempo, and rest intervals. The more specific your training requirements are, the more specific your training programme must be. This transfer of training is important if time spent in the gym is to be reflected by improved performance on the sports field or by improved body composition, a common goal of the recreational exerciser.

Overload

For the body to actually begin to adapt to training, the demands of that training must overload the system we are targeting beyond that to which it is accustomed in order to avoid a plateau in training and a lack of results.

There are two main ways to overload the body with exercise. We can either increase the actual training load, for example, by performing extra sets (increasing volume) or lifting heavier weights (increasing intensity), or we can change the exercise to one that you have not been used to and which therefore overloads your body in a different way to the existing routine.

The amount of load used can be categorised into three different groups.

- **Stimulating**. A load greater than normally used, typically resulting in a positive training adaptation.
- **Retaining**. A load sufficient to maintain training adaptations, but not great enough to bring about further changes.
- **Detraining**. A load that is not sufficient to either improve or maintain current fitness levels, leading then to a drop in performance over time.

It is important to remember that the level of load that is stimulating for a beginner will be significantly less than that needed by an experienced trainee.

Accommodation

Every time someone performs the same workout, the body learns to accommodate to it, needing less energy and effort to perform it each time, so the results lessen over time. Eventually, when the results stop coming the trainee becomes de-motivated and often gives up, as they believe the training is no longer effective. This situation can be easily remedied by supplying a fresh stimulus to the system, such as replacing a steady-state session of running with an interval training session.

Individualisation

We are all different and as such we all have unique training requirements. The use of overly dogmatic approaches to designing exercise programmes is limiting and counter-productive. A one-size-fits-all approach will achieve great results in some, average results in most, and poor results for others.

Although seemingly simple, it is amazing how commonly these principles are neglected. When they are, it almost certainly means that, no matter how creative the exercises selected, the results will be significantly limited. This is of equal importance to those who want to reduce bodyweight as it is to those seeking to improve sports performance.

The taxonomy of strength training differs from text to text and can become incredibly complicated. Let's now look at each of these different methods along with the advantages and disadvantages of each, and some suggested training applications.

Dynamic strength

Dynamic strength training has become better known as plyometrics. The term itself comes from two words where *plio* means more and *metric* means length. It is a type of training where you actually project the resistance, which may be your own bodyweight or an object, such as a medicine ball. True plyometrics, though, are those that involve a rapid lengthening of a muscle followed by a fast change into an explosive shortening. This is something commonly seen in sport, hence the popularity of this type of training amongst performance coaches.

One of the great benefits of this type of training is that training with light loads when using a barbell requires the body to actually decelerate the weight at the end of the movement to prevent injury. In contrast, plyometric training is geared around accelerating the weight at the end of the movement, making it ideal for sports where end range force is critical, such as boxing or karate.

Plyometric exercises can range from very high-intensity (depth jumps, loaded jumps, heavy medicine ball throws) to low-intensity (skipping, bounding, hopping, light medicine ball work). These types of drills are very well suited to sports that involve the need for great acceleration of bodyweight or light objects, such as basketball, volleyball, boxing, martial arts, and many field sports. They are excellent for sports where reactive ability is key as they can be used to train this ability through a wide range of drills and methods.

However, plyometrics should not be applied haphazardly. Although low intensity drills make excellent dynamic warm-ups, the more high-impact versions place great stress on joints and connective tissue (tendons and ligaments in particular) and can easily be overdone. While the drills themselves are safe and seemingly very effective, if not carefully planned and programmed they can lead to injury and nervous system fatigue.

Speed-strength method

Speed-strength activities are very similar to dynamic methods and essentially only differ in that the resistance is not normally projected or released by the trainee. The focus of speed-strength work is still very much based on the acceleration of a low weight through a sports specific pattern of movement. An example of this might be to perform a sports movement wearing a weight vest or with some type of elastic resistance attached. While it does provide

strengthening through very specific patterns of movement, there are some drawbacks. Technique must be monitored very closely. Adding greater load will almost certainly change how someone moves as their body adapts to the increased burden. Excessive weight could easily lead to the development of far from desirable movement patterns.

It is therefore advisable that this type of training is only used with trainees who have a high degree of skill in their movement patterns, and by a coach who is able to spot and correct the subtlest of technique changes during a drill.

Strength-speed method

This method involves training for situations where strength and speed are once again combined, but with strength being the central factor. It is well suited for people in sports where they have to shift a considerable weight quickly, such as rugby or judo. Olympic lifting as shown in Chapter 6 is probably the best-known example of strength-speed training; in contrast to some powerlifting movements, Olympic lifts have a high reliance on speed as well as strength.

Another type of strength-speed training involves using more simple lifts but with a lighter load (typically between 50% and 75% of maximum) accelerated at maximal velocity, sometimes using bands or chains to keep the resistance high at the end of the movement.

These types of exercises should not be used with the kind of volume that bodybuilders would use for their workouts. They place a large burden on the nervous system due to the high rate of force development, coordination, and mental toughness needed to perform them correctly. Doing too much can quickly lead to overtraining, so quality not quantity is important.

As these movements are also more complex there is an inherently greater risk of performing them incorrectly. Take time to learn the movements correctly and do not be tempted to increase the weight until the technique is perfected. When done correctly this type of training can have significant effects on the body, developing high levels of strength and power without excessive muscle growth.

Repeated effort (controlled speed) method

This system is probably the most widely used in health clubs and gyms around the country. It encompasses the training techniques most commonly used in bodybuilding and advocated for 'aesthetic' benefits over specific performance improvement. It also includes formats such as circuit training against time or for a fixed number of repetitions to either fatigue or failure.

It is most often employed for either hypertrophy (increasing muscle size) or metabolic (strength-endurance) purposes and is generally characterised by higher volumes of work, lower speed of movement, and often isolation exercises (such as bicep curls or lateral raises) designed to target individual muscles.

This is the favoured method of most recreational weight trainees, mostly due to the range of health benefits gained from the sheer amount of movement it involves, such as strengthening bones, tendons, and ligaments. It is worth remembering though, gaining size is not always beneficial and that increases in muscle size do not always transfer to improvements in performance. Bigger muscles also mean that the density of capillaries (blood vessels) within that muscle is reduced, directly affecting the ability of that muscle to carry out sustained work.

By contrast, in circuit training-type formats, where exercises are performed for many repetitions and longer durations, the adaptations favour the increase of endurance and metabolic changes rather than muscle size. This is because the muscle fibres with the greatest capacity are not sufficiently stimulated to cause hypertrophy.

This type of training is used by sports that involve high metabolic demands for repeated bouts of energy such as boxing, martial arts, football and rugby.

Maximal strength method

Maximal strength training is tough as it involves working close to your limit with every lift in a set. This is in sharp contrast to the previous method where usually only the final couple of repetitions provide that challenge.

Maximal strength training also encompasses techniques such as eccentric training and isometric training, although these are not seen often outside the most serious of weights areas. Eccentric training emphasises the lowering part of the exercise rather than the raising (or concentric) movement. It does this by using weights that are lowered under control then raised with the help of a spotter (see Chapter 3). Although it can bring about strength improvements through the high levels of muscle activation, it is also highly stressful and should be used sparingly as a training method. It is also known as negative or yielding training.

Isometric training is even less common. It also revolves around high levels of muscle activation, this time through pushing or pulling against an immovable object. A simple example of this would be an isometric squat where the trainee attempts to extend back to the start position against a bar that is either pinned into the rack, or fixed (as on a Smith machine). The

big drawback for isometric training is that strength gains only occur at the position in the movement at which you generate force. These improvements don't transfer into other angles and types of movement. High intensity isometric training involves large increases in blood pressure that are contraindicated for those with cardiovascular conditions.

Whereas the repeated effort method tends to stimulate changes in the structure and metabolism of the muscles, maximal strength methods affect most of their changes in the neural mechanisms. Due to the heavy weights involved, this type of training is best suited to multi-joint exercises such as bench press, squat, deadlifts, and overhead presses.

Using large weights is very stressful on the body so it is important that volume is well controlled and that it isn't a tool used excessively. Too much of this training is likely to lead to a drop in performance and quickly to overtraining. Performance during heavy sessions tends to fluctuate more noticeably than many other types of weight training and can be reliant on emotional state, motivation, and levels of fatigue.

Supramaximal method

Training with weights well beyond your maximum capability is dangerous and should not be practised regularly as it will swiftly lead to overtraining, poor recovery, and soreness.

Supramaximal training is often performed using partial reps (to break a sticking point in an exercise), very heavy eccentric reps (with up to 140% of normal maximum), or by using cheating movements and momentum to overcome a sticking point in the movement (such as bouncing the bar off the chest in a bench press).

This method should be used with care, and only under the guidance of a qualified strength coach. As part of a shock method of training it is one way to break a training plateau, but it can easily cause more problems than it solves if used incorrectly.

The strength deficit

As individuals we all have great potential for strength development that is often untapped. For example, we are capable of producing great strength under extreme or life-or-death situations where the nervous system is excited well beyond the levels during a workout. This is known as the strength deficit and is something we aim to improve with weight training.

Being unable to tap into our available muscle effectively during a workout means that a proportion of the muscle simply isn't being trained. If a strength deficit is large and training methods are focused on commonly used approaches (higher volumes, lower loads, 8–15 repetitions) then eventually the trainee will plateau, unable to lift any more weight. To improve this, training must focus more on lifting greater loads with lower volume and greater speed, which will stimulate the nervous system to a far greater extent bringing increases in both maximal and sub-maximal strength.

Measuring our own strength deficit is difficult, but an awareness of it is an important reminder to include training methods that stimulate the nervous system as well as increase muscle size.

Overtraining

It is important to be aware of the signs and symptoms of overtraining so that the dedicated trainees can learn to recognise it and adjust their training accordingly.

When the effects of fatigue begin to chronically overtake the fitness benefits, performance starts to suffer and there is a risk of overtraining. It can be tricky to balance as we have already established that some degree of stress is necessary to elicit a training effect.

The most common type of overtraining syndrome that people suffer from is called Basedowic or B-overtraining and its symptoms are shown below.
• Tendency to get tired easily
• Increased need for sleep
• Reduction in work capacity (sometimes severe performance drops)
• Constant feelings of stiffness, soreness, or fatigue
• Longer recovery times between workouts
• Nervousness, anxiety, and loss of motivation

Overtraining is usually related to sheer volumes of training, or to prolonged periods of high intensity training without adequate recovery. Immediate treatment should be a sharp reduction in training volume rather than simply a reduction in intensity.

EQUIPMENT

2

The variety of equipment available can be overwhelming. This chapter looks at the major types of equipment.

Barbells or dumbbells?

Barbells and dumbbells are the two principal training tools that are used for free weight training and each comes with its own pros and cons. Barbells offer greater potential for loading than dumbbells, enabling you to move greater weights during maximal efforts. The bilateral nature of a typical barbell exercise allows maximal effort to be applied through the bar with each side of the body providing a counterbalance to the force produced by the contra-lateral limb.

However, in everyday life and sport it is rare for activities to involve both hands being fixed to a bar and working in the identical plane and range of movement. Recreating this unilateral challenge requires equipment that allows each limb to operate independently of the other, and that is where dumbbells come in. Dumbbells also make it possible to load the body asymmetrically placing a far greater demand for stability through the kinetic chain.

Barbells are usually purchased as part of a weights set, along with the necessary collars and a range of weights, and vary hugely in price. Dumbbells also come in a wide range of types from the chrome headed types through to the rubber hexagonal-shaped variety. The hexagonal-shaped varieties offer greater versatility than the conventional types as they can be used on the floor without rolling around.

Kettlebells

A kettlebell (or girya) is basically a big lump of iron with a handle on it, which traditionally comes in weights called poods. One pood weighs 16kg, although they are available in a wide range of different weights. Workout formats usually involve a large number of repetitions (often up to 30 or 40) of double and single arm whole-body movements, many based on the Olympic lifts of the snatch and clean. While there is no disputing the challenging aspect of these routines (such as the 10 minutes of constant snatches with either arm used by the US Secret Service as a fitness test), their results are generally thought of in terms of density (excellent for general conditioning and fat loss) rather than intensity (essential for increasing strength and explosive power). There are different variations of exercises possible with the kettlebell, many that are highly challenging, such as the Turkish get up. Exercises with the kettlebell also challenge the grip and strength at different points in the movement and the weight, located at a different point to conventional dumbbells, also makes for extra work. Although there is certainly more substance to kettlebell training than many other fitness systems, it is simply another method that can get great results under the right conditions. Technique is important with the kettlebell to avoid injury to the wrists and forearms so find a qualified trainer to help you get started. It is great fun and sure to challenge anyone from the novice to the hardened training veteran. See some kettlebell-specific exercises in Chapter 6.

Powerbags

Powerbags are the modern day gym version of the sandbag. They are a tough canvas-type bag with two straps, filled with sand to various weights. Powerbags have the advantage of being safe to use indoors and outdoors for throwing drills. As the section on bands and chains shows, developing force at different points on the strength curve is particularly useful for sports that involve throwing or releasing a weight. They have been a popular training tool among rugby teams, due in part to their durability and versatility when used in drills to replicate game situations and movements.

Medicine balls

The trusty medicine ball has been a popular training tool for many years and still remains a very versatile piece of kit for explosive catch and release drills. Training these drills focuses on the development of explosive strength or speed-strength, where the emphasis is on moving the weight at the greatest velocity possible. When training, too heavy a ball can compromise strength gains, so select yours carefully. Remember, if the intention is to improve the rate of force development and explosive speed, then you should be able to move the weight at great velocity.

Another variant on the common medicine ball is the powerball, which is just a medicine ball with handles. These are not suitable for throwing or catching drills because of the risk of injury to the fingers from the handles. They are more useful in core training or dynamic warm-up drills.

Stability balls and other instability equipment

If there is one certainty about just about any fitness centre in the land, it is that it will contain at least one stability ball (also known as a Swiss ball). Stability balls usually are sized between 45–75cm and are used to create an unstable environment on which to train.

As always in the fitness industry, opinions are fairly well split on the subject; I think that in general instability devices such as these are overused when trying to improve strength and body composition. Devices such as stability balls do have a large part to play in the rehabilitation process helping to facilitate the return to movement from a highly stabilised environment to a more functional and variable one. The validity of unstable surfaces (stability balls, Bosu, DynaDiscs, Core Board, etc) in rehabilitation or for those with poor motor function is clearer than for strength training per se, with an abundance of research supporting its use. Some studies even found it to be of use in correcting muscular imbalances. Injury damages proprioception (the way we sense position and react to changes in movement) and unstable surfaces offer a range of challenges to the motor system that stimulate improvement and effectively teach the body to react to dynamic changes in the environment. For this reason some instability devices can be used as part of a warm-up or activation exercise to encourage the 'firing' of stabilisers, effectively waking the muscles up with a greater neurological challenge in preparation for the main exercise.

When it comes to strength development though, things are slightly different. With the increased use of devices like the Bosu and stability balls in strength training they often used instead of the conventional bench in an effort to achieve better spinal stabilisation challenge or muscle activity. However, recent research from America has shown that unstable surface training (such as using an inflatable disc under the foot) can potentially decrease performance and reduce power gains – not what you want if you are an athlete!

Researchers cannot even seem to agree, for example, on whether the use of a stability ball to replace a bench in a strength training exercise is beneficial or not but the simple rule here is that if your aim is to challenge the body's stabilisers then unstable surfaces such as a stability ball can help to achieve that through a range of exercises. Adding instability needs to be done with care to prevent you from adopting undesirable patterns of movement in an effort to cope with the increased challenge; form needs to be closely watched.

If your aim is to develop strength, hypertrophy, or the ability to generate increased levels of force in a certain pattern of movement then adding instability may merely reduce the level of intensity at which you can lift. It also encourages very slow and deliberate, sometimes tentative, movement. This is another unwanted adaptation for anyone wanting to improve speed, strength, or power. When it comes to the efficacy of these devices for sports performance it should also be remembered that the principle of specificity applies to training and that during sport we move but the ground underneath us stays still, which questions the crossover of these very unstable exercises to sports movement. In particular, instability can be a valid tool for the upper body, where it is used less

often, as it is in the upper body where unstable and asymmetric forces are often applied. An excellent way to generate instability is through the use of unilateral exercises or asymmetrically loaded movements.

It is more commonly accepted now that some degree of unstable training can be beneficial to overall performance (perhaps as part of an unloading phase or back off period when the goal is to reduce joint loading and overall force), though it should be remembered that many of these devices such as wobble boards and inflatable discs originated in the physio room for those with injury, not in the weights room for those wanting to improve performance. Manufacturers who make claims for the performance-enhancing effects of this equipment often do so with little actual proof or justification.

Weight training belts

The weight belt seems to be a bit of a fashion accessory in health clubs, despite the fact that the large number of people who use them have absolutely no need for them at all.

Opinions vary on the value of using the belt. Nature has actually given us our very own weight belt in the form of abdominal musculature that runs down, around, and across our mid-section enabling us to create stability when we lift up weights. It is our abdominals that work to create what is known as intra-abdominal pressure (IAP), which helps stabilise the trunk and provide dynamic stability during lifting tasks.

Although weight belts tend to be thought of as an aid to the back, how they actually help people to lift more weight is by giving the abdominals something to press against to create greater levels of IAP. A study in 1999 showed that wearing an abdominal belt during a laboratory task actually caused *less* activation of the spinal erectors in the lumbar region during spinal flexion. This is certainly not a conducive motor pattern to develop for spinal health.

So, should you actually be wearing one? Well, there are instances, such as when attempting a maximal lift, when it may be warranted. However, you should certainly *not* learn to lift with a weight belt or wear one just as a course of habit, as sustained use could have a detrimental effect on spinal stability and abdominal coordination. The chances are that if you are healthy and not trying to break any powerlifting records then you have little to gain from spending money on a new weightlifting belt and you would be better off focusing on developing superior lifting technique instead. If you already use one, then it is a good idea to work on effectively using your abdominals without wearing a belt. If you regularly lift heavy weights with a belt, take time to work yourself off it, as your body may not know how to stabilise effectively without it.

Straps, wraps, and other lifting gear

As well as the commonly-seen weight lifting belt, there are also a wide range of different straps, wraps, bench shirts, and squat suits. Most of this kit has little application to the everyday weight trainee and is specific to the sport of powerlifting, where the use of gear can greatly increase the amount of weight that a competitor can shift.

Much of this equipment works on a similar principle as the belt, placing the body tightly into a restricted range of movement specific to the demands of the exercise. The use of a heavy weight then stretches the garment through the movement providing a greatly increased level of elastic recoil at the sticking point and enabling the lifter to move a weight far greater than would normally be possible.

The actual application of this type of kit, such as special shirts for bench pressing or suits worn for squatting, often raises some strong opinion and there are many who feel that its use is tantamount to cheating and is not a true reflection of the person's actual strength. Despite this, however, its use has come as the sport of powerlifting has evolved, in much the same way as the tennis racquet has improved to allow the ball to be hit harder. Lifting gear is now an integral part of the sport and seems set to remain that way. Lifters will also commonly tightly wrap their knee and wrist joints to provide added stability and to allow the generation of maximal muscle force with little consideration for its actual direction or balance of application. As with several of their more specialised exercises (such as box squats) a full exploration of this is well beyond the scope of this book.

Wrist straps, though, are more commonly seen in the gym and can be useful when the grip is starting to fatigue. Use of a pair of straps reduces the need for grip strength during pulling movements by transferring the strain onto the looped strap at the wrist. Bodybuilders whose main goal is to overload a specific pattern of movement to a high level of fatigue commonly use them. This can often place a large burden on grip strength, particularly if performing two pulling movements during a workout. The most popular exercises for their use are deadlifts, bent-over rows, and chin-ups, although they can also be used with dumbbells during sets of lunges, for example. In general, strength coaches would not advocate use of straps, as this is a classic example of how to further limit performance. This is of little concern to the average bodybuilder, but should be of prime importance for those for whom grip strength is necessary for their ability to express total strength. Instead, focus should be given to incorporating dedicated grip training into other workouts where the grip does not suffer such fatigue in an effort to bring it into line with the strength of the movements being performed.

Bands and chains

There are two key areas that provide good reason for the introduction of band and chains into certain resistance training programmes.

Firstly, we have the problem of deceleration when lifting weights to develop explosive power. One way around this problem is to use ballistic-type training where the weight is actually released.

Bands and chains offer another solution but pose another problem that may be encountered when using free weights. During any given free weights exercise we are only actually as strong as we are at the weakest point of the movement due to the effects of gravity and biomechanics. By adding bands or chains to a movement, the resistance increases as the exercise would normally get easier. The band stretches and grows tighter as it is lengthened through a lift. Because of the elastic nature of the band, not only is it increasing the effort needed to push the bar upwards, it is also actively trying to contract and pull the bar downwards. This effect creates far greater eccentric stress to the muscle when lowering the weight, as you will need to increase muscle activity to lower the bar under control. Alternatively, this effect can be used to create a plyometric-type training effect, where the muscle generates an explosive concentric contraction immediately after a rapid eccentric one. The science supports this approach with a study in 2006 from the *Journal of Strength and Conditioning Research* concluding that the addition of bands (accounting for 20% of the total resistance) when working at 85% of 1RM (repetition maximum) can significantly improve peak power and peak force compared to free weights alone.

Weight releasers

Weight releasers allow the use of a greater weight for the eccentric part of a movement. Simple in design, they consist of a hook – the weights are attached at one end, while the hooked end is placed over the barbell. During the lowering phase the weight is increased, then at the bottom of the movement the weights are released from the bar and the concentric part of the movement is performed with the lighter load. As eccentric strength is always greater than concentric strength, development of it is limited by what we can lift after we have lowered it. There are other methods such as having a partner provide assistance during the concentric portion, or by pushing down on the bar to increase the resistance during the eccentric phase. Weight releasers simply offer a more quantitative method for doing this.

Sledgehammer training and other methods

It is worth briefly mentioning several systems of training that are either being reinvented or adapted from an existing method to provide more options to the strength training coach and personal trainer.

Recently there has been a renewed interest in strongman style training with a departure from the use of the conventional gym-based equipment to the lifting and dragging of a wide variety of heavy objects, such as weighted sleds, tyre flipping, logs, rope, and chains. Along with kettlebells and Indian club training, people are now even using sledgehammers to improve their conditioning.

Used wisely there is no reason why any of this equipment should not produce some great results although as we have already seen – randomly applying different training means, without giving any thought to why, is not likely to lead to optimal adaptations. Many of these adapted and improvised activities also greatly increase the risk of injury to novice trainees who may have poor movement or muscle function. In general, methods such as strongman type training are specialised and should only be undertaken after a period of general physical preparation to build the essential strength and technique required for safe execution. Although these methods may lack the quantitative element that comes with adding precise incremental amounts of load that is possible with weights and dumbbells, it is an approach that develops strength and should not be overlooked as a training method.

Home gym essentials

Gyms and health clubs are not for everyone. For whatever reason, many choose to do their training at home. Creating your own home gym will largely be dependent on space and what type of training you plan to do. Those wanting to undertake some fairly serious strength training will need a reasonable amount of space – a single car garage with a high enough roof is usually sufficient. For those looking for something a little more basic,

it is reasonably cheap and easy to buy some kit to use in a spare room or outside.

If you are thinking of setting up a home gym in your garage then here are the essentials that I would recommend for a multitude of exercises:
• Squat rack or power rack
• Olympic bar and collars
• Olympic dumbbell handles
• Olympic weight plate set
• Adjustable bench
• Stability ball
• TRX system (see below)

On the other hand, if you are looking for something even simpler, more affordable, or smaller then here is my recommended list for the spare room:
• Adjustable dumbbells (such as those made by Powerbloc)
• Stability ball
• Mat
• Exercise bands or tubing

Obviously the less equipment you have the more you will need to use your imagination to keep coming up with routines that are varied enough to be both challenging and interesting. The TRX system is a relatively new system and is an excellent low-cost conditioning tool that relies on bodyweight as its resistance. This versatile, easy to store piece of kit can be fixed to a wide range of points and is ideal for a space that cannot be constantly reserved for exercise. It is simply a webbing strap with handles on each end that can varied in length to perform a wide range of exercises for the whole body.

SAFETY

3

It goes without saying that when it comes to weight training there is always an inherent risk of injury, although as in occupations and hobbies, most injuries can be avoided by observing some simple rules in the weights room. By paying attention to how you train, you will get both a safer and more effective training session.

Spotting and training safely

In an ideal world we would always train with someone to spot us. The responsibilities of the spotter during a workout are shown below.
• Add encouragement and motivation
• Monitor technique and give feedback
• Assist in completion of a repetition
• Assist during eccentric/negative training
• Count tempo, rhythm, rest, or repetitions
• Unload bar during drop sets/strip sets
• Summon help if required

Of course, the lifter can do many these things on their own, so the main responsibility of a spotter is primarily one of safety. For maximum safety, particularly when attempting maximal lifts, it would be ideal to have two people spotting, although this isn't always possible outside a dedicated lifting club. Often it will be a case of asking someone on a rest period or a duty gym instructor to help you out, in which case remember the following guidelines.
• Is the spotter actually strong enough to help you? If you are planning to attempt a 300kg squat then there is little point asking the 65kg aerobics instructor to come and help you out. A spotter **must** be strong enough to provide assistance to the lifter at any given point in the lift.
• During squats, two is always better than one. Remember that if there is only one spotter then they will only be able to provide assistance if you fail, they will not be in a position to actually lift the weight clear.
• The spotter should know how many repetitions you are planning to achieve and be instructed not to assist until the bar has stopped moving.
• Encouragement from a spotter is good and can help you to achieve your target amount of repetitions.
• The spotter should always be in a position to assist by being attentive to your movements at all times.
• The spotter should not stand in your eyeline. Trying to attempt a maximal lift in the bench press is difficult when your spotter's crotch is hanging over your face.

Remember, if you are training alone, at home for example, then it is wise not to attempt maximal lifts or to perform sets until you can do no more and to always keep your mobile phone within arm's reach, just in case of an accident.

Some simple rules of safe lifting

We can summarise some good lifting practices with a simple set of rules below, most of which should be common sense for most people.

Always use collars on the bars

Collars prevent the weight plates from moving on the bar, which can destabilise the lift and lead to serious injury. To stay safe always collar your weights on every lift.

Never attempt a maximal lift without a spotter capable of assisting if you get stuck

If you are in the gym and planning to train to failure, ask someone to spot for you, or at the very least work from a bench where you can rack the bar at any height.

If training at home or on your own in the gym, keep a phone close to hand in case of accident

For those with gyms in their shed or garage this is an essential rule to follow. Always keep a phone within arm's reach in case of an accident.

Always unload heavy bars evenly when racked

Unloading the bar unevenly results in the barbell detaching itself fairly explosively from the rack, usually accompanied by a large and embarrassing noise. To avoid this ensure that you load and unload bars evenly when they are racked.

Clear your weights away as you go

Weight room etiquette seems to be largely non-existent in most places, but that is no excuse for leaving your bar or weights on the gym floor. It only takes a few seconds to replace them and prevents them from becoming a significant hazard to others. Not only that, but it is extremely frustrating to have to clear up after someone else's workout before you can get on with your own.

Never train through pain or injury

Pain is usually a sign that something is not working the way it should and by repeatedly continuing to load that problem area you are asking for trouble. Many chronic problems, such as shoulder impingement, often start with a little pain before getting steadily worse. To avoid long-term problems get all injuries checked out, don't train through painful movements, and schedule regular transition weeks into your training where volume is reduced. It is a good idea to do this one week a month.

Never sacrifice quality for quantity

Never compromise the quality of your workout in order to simply get more reps or sets out. Poor quality sets (where weight has to be drastically reduced to allow completion, or cheating movements are used) are little more than a waste of time in the gym. If you are severely fatigued on one exercise then simply drop it and move on to the next one.

Always pick up and lower the bar with good form

Injuries often happen when lifting or lowering a weight to the floor. There is little point lifting with excellent form for the set number of repetitions and then putting the bar down with terrible form. Remember, the exercise starts the moment you put your hands on the bar.

Take phone calls outside the weights area

Making phone calls while in the weights area is not only disruptive to your own workout, but also to others. Training requires mental focus and a degree of intensity not possible if you are taking phone calls between sets. Turn your phone off while you are in the gym.

Train in appropriate clothing

Training clothing should allow you to move comfortably through all planes of movement and again should reflect your attitude towards your workout. You don't have to be wearing the very latest in dry-fit spandex but you should be using both appropriate footwear and sports training clothing.

Sit down before you fall down if you feel faint

A big set of squats can really take it out of you, so, should you start to feel a little light-headed, lie down before you fall down. This can also be the case if you have done a lot of metabolic work and then not cooled down adequately. A simple remedy is to lie on the floor with your feet elevated on a bench or stability ball.

Always warm up thoroughly before attempting maximals

It goes without saying that you should warm-up before you train. If you are planning to lift free weights at maximal or close to maximal level then you should work up to those weights using a progression of lighter weights. To prevent excessive fatigue and lactate accumulation, never complete more than 6 reps as part of a warm-up set. An example of a warm-up for a bench press session of triples would look like this (assuming you bench 100kg for 3RM).

Warm-up sets

5 Reps @ 40kg
4 Reps @ 60kg
3 Reps @ 80kg
2 Reps @ 90kg
1 Rep @ 95kg

Of course, some people might need a couple of sets fewer than this. Remember a warm-up gets you prepared for the workout, it isn't the actual workout and therefore should not fatigue you for your work sets. Generally the greater the weight you plan to do your work sets at – the more warm-up sets you will need.

Breathing

How to breathe during various exercises is an area still lacking in research and somewhat equivocal as to the best approach. The general advice is often that breath-holding during exertion should be avoided at all costs. However, key texts in both rehabilitation and in weight lifting technique both highlight the different applications of breathing according to the task in hand.

When you to bend over and pick up a pair of shoes, the chances are you would do it with little consideration of how you were breathing. In contrast, if you had to give your car a push start then it is likely you would take a big breath, fill your lungs, hold it, and then push for all you were worth – two very different techniques.

The reason for this is that to push your car you need to generate a large amount of force to overcome the inertia of the car and get it moving. This level of exertion requires a high degree of stability to transfer the energy from the floor up to the car and therefore high levels of IAP (intra-abdominal pressure). Without this stability effective force transfer would simply not be possible. Achieving this through breath-holding is known as a Valsalva manoeuvre and is also used by other athletes during a wide range of maximal effort tasks. Conversely picking up your shoes is a relatively low load task and does not require high levels of IAP to complete.

The danger of straining against a closed airway is the deleterious rise in blood pressure that could be particularly hazardous for anyone with cardiovascular health problems, for whom the Valsalva manoeuvre is contraindicated. So, what should you be doing with your breathing during exercise?

It would at first seem simple – just don't hold your breath – and this is the advice given as a general rule. The only problem is that consciously not holding your breath while trying to lift a heavy weight is likely to greatly increase the risk of a serious injury by greatly reducing IAP and increasing the strain on to the more vulnerable parts of the lumbar spine.

So, breathing should be appropriate to the level of challenge involved in the lift itself. Advising someone to try to breathe normally during a set of 3RM squats is close to idiotic, while it should be encouraged during more functional activities. Spinal stability expert and renowned bio-mechanist Stuart McGill advises in his book *Ultimate Back Fitness and Performance*, 'An important feature of stable and functional backs is the ability to co-contract the abdominal wall independent of any lung ventilation patterns and that training to a specific exertion pattern may not be advantageous for athletic performance'.

Injury prevention in free weight training

While training with free weights is likely to make a positive impression on your health and general well-being, it does have the potential to make things worse if done poorly. However, done right it can actually protect against injury by strengthening potential problem areas and helping to address muscle imbalances caused through sport, illness, injury, or the simple stresses and strains of everyday life. This benefit of resistance training has become known as prehabilitation, although really it is what every free weight training programme should be aiming for. A full and complete review of injuries – their causes and prevention – is well beyond the scope of this book, but this is one area where further learning is definitely worth while. Some of the most awkward and annoying injuries sustained when lifting weights can often be avoided by simply testing or modifying your technique, along with a healthy

dose of common sense. The information here is **not** designed as a diagnostic tool or guarantee of an injury-free future. Instead it should help you to spot the first signs of trouble and to take action to prevent it becoming a problem.

In the weights room injuries occur through one of three ways: trauma/accidental, faulty loading, and overloading. It is important to remember that injuries are also individual. What is injurious to one person, might form the crux of another's training programme. Similarly, what is appropriate for the advanced trainee would probably not be wise for the novice. This blurs the line between what is safe and unsafe, balanced and unbalanced, too little or too much and goes to show that training is far from an exact science in many respects.

Red flags

Red flags are signs that something is not right and that you should stop exercising and get expert guidance before you go any further.

If you experience any of the following then consult a medical professional before continuing with your exercise regime.
- Radiating pain
- Numbness/tingling
- Loss of range of motion
- Loss of function
- Swelling
- Night pains
- Chest pain/shortness of breath/wheezing
- Open wounds

Make a note of your symptoms, how long they lasted, and what might have triggered them.

If you are unsure as to whether or not it is safe for you to start a programme of weight training then ask yourself the questions below. If you can honestly answer no to each one, then it is a good indicator that you can begin a programme of moderate exercise without too many concerns. This is the bare minimum though and if you have any reason for concern or are aged over 45 it is a good idea to get a check up first.

1. Has your doctor ever told you that you have a heart problem?
2. Do you feel pain in the chest during physical activity?
3. In the past month have you had chest pain when not doing physical activity?
4. Do you often feel faint or have spells of dizziness?
5. Do you have a bone or joint problem that could be made worse through a change in activity levels?
6. Are you currently being prescribed drugs for blood pressure or a heart condition?
7. Are you over 65 and not accustomed to exercise?
8. Are you diabetic?
9. Are you pregnant?
10. Do you smoke?

Pain can come from many sources and in some cases without any detectable cause. The pain most people associate with exercise is the build up of metabolic substances in the muscle that can cause burning sensations and even nausea and light headedness – this soon passes with either a reduction or halt in the exercise. Pain of any other sort should almost always be avoided. If you are in pain before you even start your workout then you need to take some action before hitting the weights. Whether chronic or acute, pain is a sign that something is not quite right in the body. This can range from a muscle strain through to something more serious.

Is there such a thing as a 'bad exercise'?

There is rarely such a thing as a 'bad exercise' – just a bad choice of exercise.

Given that an exercise has to create a certain amount of stress to create an adaptation, there will always be the potential for any exercise to cause someone problems. So, how can you be sure that the exercises you are doing are not harmful? Ask yourself the following questions about any given exercise.

- Is the exercise necessary? It is not necessary for everyone to Olympic lift, or to bench press, or even to do Pilates for optimum health. If the exercise is not needed for you to get to your goals, do you really need to be doing it?
- Is it appropriate? So, you have established that you need to do some kind of exercise for your chosen goal, now you must ask if your choice is really an appropriate choice for the reps, sets, and tempo selected? Also, is it appropriate to the given training phase and environment?
- Is it effective? Will the exercise do what you want it to do and be an effective use of your time? Similarly ask yourself if the exercise gives you enough bang for your buck? Does it provide a sufficient level of challenge to stimulate the changes you are hoping for?
- Is it safe? Finally, the big question, is it actually safe to do this? If it seems inherently dangerous then it might not be a good idea. If you are unsure then find a trained professional and ask their advice. Remember, just because you see someone else doing it in the gym does not necessarily make it a safe choice for you.

If you can answer all of these questions with a confident yes then you are probably not going too far wrong.

Muscle balance, posture and position

Although posture is one of the latest trends that the industry has focused on, it is a valid area to consider in relation to injury prevention. In relation to weight training specifically, problems occur when people with certain postural deviations begin programmes of exercise that have the potential to worsen their posture, rather than to improve it. Many people now have postural problems that can inhibit good movement and heavily favour flexion over extension. When they begin to train with weights there is then a natural desire to perform the movements they feel strongest in – those of flexion, rather than extension – rather than targeting weakened muscles.

A full review of posture and its effects is well out of the scope of this book, but by being aware of your own posture you can learn to both pick appropriate exercises and monitor your own position more effectively during training so refer to the texts in the bibliography for more information. A good trainer should always perform some sort of postural assessment before designing a plan of exercise, as this ensures that any existing imbalances will not be made any worse through training.

Stretching – does it prevent injury?

There is a perception that stretching is a necessary and integral part of injury prevention, although when it comes to weight training it may be that this belief is not entirely true. The vast differences between individual needs of flexibility make large-scale study of set protocols somewhat unreliable. There is no research to corroborate the use of stretching before a weight training workout to prevent injury, and there is, in fact, a negative relationship in certain cases between flexibility and injury, particularly in the back. For performance, an amount of stiffness and recoil is necessary in the muscles. There is evidence that stretching before weight training can reduce the ability to produce power and damages coordination. Static stretching in particular raises parasympathetic nervous system activity, the opposite of what is needed before training. If you rely on explosive dynamic movements such as jumping or throwing, stretching should be undertaken with care as working beyond your range of movement may decrease elastic recoil and actually worsen physical performance.

It is clear that flexibility work is an important aspect of fitness, and should be approached with the same level of needs analysis as the rest of a training programme, as individual needs vary greatly. For some, mobility work should take precedence in their training programme to help to develop optimal movement. As part of a warm-up routine, active movements through the range of movement to be worked are more effective at preparing the body for activity than static stretching, whereas static stretching can be employed as part of a cool-down (or better still as a completely separate entity) to greater effect. The exception to this is where stretching is employed to achieve an optimal range of movement at a particular area, or help to correct clear muscular imbalances. For example, those with tight pectoral muscles (scapula protractors) can benefit from stretching these before a pulling workout that strengthens the shoulder retractors. It should also be remembered that increasing mobility in a joint will also raise the need for stability there to ensure joint health, hence the importance of training through a full range of movement.

The shoulder – should you be lifting overhead or even pressing at all?

One area that is well worth considering when preparing a training programme is the shoulder. It is prone to injury in people who lift free weights, and is the most inherently unstable structure in the body. Although the shoulder has great mobility and range of movement, this also makes it prone to instability and injury. Part of the reason for this is that the upper arm (humerus) does not locate in the joint in the same way as the hip joint and is therefore reliant on the stabilising actions of many different muscles to maintain a healthy position during movement. As soon as these muscles stop operating correctly, things start to go wrong.

A lack of stability around the shoulder can lead to a vast range of conditions developing, though by far the most common amongst people using weights is called Impingement Syndrome, which occurs when the position of the scapula and humerus are not at the best for movement, causing tissues to be trapped in the space between the two. This painful condition is surprisingly common, but preventable with care. Some of these conditions can also be confusing, as overused muscles develop trigger points (isolated muscle adhesions that are extremely tender to the touch) that send pain to other parts of the shoulder or upper arm. If you suffer from trigger points then you should consult a soft-tissue specialist as they can be eliminated through massage or active release to allow optimal movement.

There are some simple tests you can do to help you judge whether your shoulder mechanics are at their best or not. If you test positive for any of the tests below then you should correct this before venturing into too much overhead lifting or pressing movements. For most of these you will need the help of a friend, family member, or training partner. The shoulder is very complex and as such there are no specific remedies shown for these tests as the possible root causes are too varied. You should simply use them as guidelines as to whether or not you have less than optimal shoulder function.

Supine shoulder position

Lie on the floor at home and get someone to take a photo of you from your head. This test tells us about the position of your shoulders and in particular whether or not the *pectoralis minor* is short and tight.

Your shoulders should lie comfortably against the floor with less than an inch from the floor to the tip of your shoulder. Interestingly, people with short pec minors also tend to have short and tight abdominals, which should also be stretched. The tendency is to work the abdominals more, making the whole problem worse and highlighting how poor choices of abdominal work can contribute to shoulder injuries.

Supine shoulder flexion

This next simple test focuses on two of the big muscles of the upper body, the *pectoralis major* and the *latissimus dorsi*. These tend to shorten through poor programming choices and excessive use of exercises that favour the internal rotators of the shoulder rather than the externals (bench presses and chin-ups being two examples). Shortness of these muscles is the most common movement impairment seen in the shoulder.

Lie on your back on the floor with your feet flat and your hips and knees flexed. Your pelvis should be rotated back with the lumbar spine flat on the floor.

Extend both your arms overhead with your palms facing upwards. Ask a friend to take a picture from above and behind.

If your arms are unable to rest on the floor along their entire length, this indicates short and tight chest muscles (*pectoralis*). If your elbows deviate out to the sides, causing your arms to bend then this indicates tight lats. For optimal movement your arms should both rest on the floor without any arching of the back or twisting of the ribcage.

Back scratch test

This test for the shoulder gives a good idea as to any rotational limitations of the muscles around the joint. As with the other tests you ideally need the help of someone else.

First measure the length of your hand from the crease of the wrist to the point of your longest finger. Make a fist with each hand with the thumb inside. Raise one arm behind your back overhead, while reaching behind your back on the other side with the other arm.

If you cannot get your fists within one hand's length of each other then you need to find out what is restricting this. It can be caused by a variety of factors and it is best to get checked out before you start. Be aware that some people with high levels of hypertrophy may find this test difficult through nothing other than sheer muscle size. In that case a prone shoulder rotation test is more appropriate.

The shoulder can be a baffling joint at the best of times but some people simply are not built for overhead lifting, through osseous (bony) restrictions such as a hooked acromion or stiff thoracic spine. For those lucky sorts, adaptations can easily be used rather than simply crashing away with a behind neck barbell press until they can't lift their arms anymore. To help

you stay free of shoulder pain, here are some simple pieces of advice to follow.

- Good shoulder function is directly related to the ability of the shoulder muscles to keep the head of the humerus in the right place during movement. Pay attention to the position you are in during exercise to ensure this happens.
- If it hurts, then stop doing it, as it will only get worse with repeated poor movement.
- If you have less than optimal function at the shoulder, then stick to safer choices of exercise and avoid those that may make it worse, such as flared elbow bench press, behind neck presses, and lateral raises with medial rotation (turning the palms down).
- Balance push movements with pulls (protraction with retraction) and presses with vertical pulls (elevation with depression) and internal rotation with external. If you sit at a desk for most of the day, then use a 2:1 ratio of rowing to pressing movements in your exercise programmes.
- Work on improving thoracic extension and pay attention to your posture (not just in the gym, but also at work). If you sit at a desk all day, then take care with shoulder work, favouring pulling and external rotation patterns over all others.
- Don't worry about a 'shoulders' day in the gym – for most people this is unnecessary. Instead focus on movements that allow your shoulder to work naturally in all three planes. Remember, the shoulder gets a lot of use when you work the front and back of the body as well.
- Avoid crunches and too much forward flexion work – this just adds to thoracic flexion issues and makes life even harder for the shoulder.
- Warm the shoulder joint up thoroughly before **any** upper body work using active mobilisation work and warm-up sets.

Warming up – getting ready for free weight training

A solid warm-up is an important part of any athlete's training programme, and should be the same for anyone before performing their working sets with free weights. Some of the many benefits an adequate warm-up can bring are:

- Improved movement patterns and better coordination
- Increased blood flow to the muscles to deliver essential energy substrates
- Preparation of the nervous system for increased activity
- Speedier muscle contraction and relaxation
- Increased mental focus and preparation
- Increased muscle temperature
- Improved joint mobility and movement

The accepted method of warming up consists of a generalised approach followed by a more specific section where efforts are dedicated to more direct preparation for the working sets ahead. With free weights you have many options; I recommend the following.

- Mobilisation of key joints – focusing in particular on the thoracic spine, shoulders, and hips.
- **If needed**, stretching of any identified restrictions in movement. (A variety of methods can be used ranging from static stretching to PNF, soft-tissue release, and active-isolated work.)
- Lightly loaded movement pattern preparation (active flexibility work)
- Warm-up sets
- Work sets

This may seem a lot, but in reality it needn't take very long at all. As with all other exercise programming, your warm-up should be progressive and individualised in the same way as the rest of your programme. Many people simply use lightly loaded movements through a full range of motion as an adequate warm-up, while others may require a longer routine with a little more time dedicated to specific areas. It is important to remember that the focus of a warm-up is preparation for the main work and that a warm-up should not create fatigue that will compromise performance later. Some ideas for mobilisation and active flexibility exercises are shown below.

- Head turns and tilts
- Shoulder shrugs
- Arm circles
- Arm swings – vertical and horizontal
- Cuban press
- PNF patterns (spiral, diagonal movements across the body)
- Thoracic flexion/extension (cats and dogs)
- Trunk twists
- Dynamic leg swings – forward/back – side/side
- Static lunges
- Toe touch squats

Restoration – the importance of recovery to health

The importance of getting good recovery is one that is usually overlooked by all but the full-time athlete. However, the time after your gym visit is one of the most critical – even more so if you have been there to lift weights. Recovery can affect just about any system in the body from our hormones, through to our reaction time and should apply to three main areas: physical recovery, medical recovery, and psychological recovery. How and where you use different types of recovery is largely down to your own resources, time, and budget. While some recovery methods are more general and often used as a reward for a completed volume of training, more immediate concerns are important. There is little point following a hard weights workout by skipping food and going out drinking. Post-workout nutrition is key for good results and a combination of essential amino acids with some carbohydrate is a good start. Many post-workout recovery drinks provide this in a simple to make form.

By incorporating your recovery means into your training programme you are allowing time to let your body adapt to the stress of the workout. This is critical to improved performance and therefore should always be a consideration in your training regime.

Delayed onset muscle soreness (DOMS)

It is a fairly safe bet that once you get into free weight training you will start to feel some soreness. This is *normal* and should not panic you greatly. In particular, you will likely experience a phenomenon known as delayed onset muscle soreness or DOMS. DOMS normally sets in the day after a training session, but it may be at its worst two or even three days afterwards, depending on the type of training you did.

Some of the common symptoms of DOMS include tenderness, pain, restricted range of motion, inflammation and a temporary loss of performance. Although we can't be sure of the physiological reasons for DOMS, what we do know is that certain types of training tend to cause greater levels of it than others. In particular, eccentric training has the greatest potential for DOMS, along with plyometric and ballistic methods (such as jump squats).

Treatment of DOMS is tricky, as many conventional approaches such as ice, stretching, homeopathy and ultrasound seem to be ineffective. Some reduction in reported symptoms has been shown with the use of NSAIDs

(non-steroidal anti-inflammatory drugs, such as Ibuprofen). One of the simplest ways to ease the soreness, however, is with physical activity. DOMS is one of the reasons that split programmes are favoured by many, rather than continual use of whole-body workouts, as this allows the sore area time to recover. A simple way to get around this is to alternate upper and lower body workouts.

It is important to mention here the role of the personal trainer and strength coach. They are not there to diagnose or treat injuries as that is the realm of a skilled physiotherapist, surgeon, or similar health professional. The role of the trainer is to work with the appropriate healthcare professional to design a programme of exercise that is suitable and may aid in recovery. Sometimes this process can be of particular use in helping recovery, while in others it may have little effect beyond a psychological and more general health benefit.

Lack of recovery, imbalanced training programmes, overuse, excessive volume, and inappropriate exercises, however, are the remit of a trainer or coach and also the responsibility of the trainee.

Take some time to examine your own exercise programme before you get started and give the same kind of attention to your technique while you are actually training and you will go a long way to preventing injury.

Finding a personal trainer/strength trainer

Research from both America and Australia has shown that those who resistance trained under direct supervision made greater gains in maximal strength and had better levels of exercise adherence than those training unsupervised.

The modern personal trainer possesses a wide range of different skill sets with many specialising in post-rehabilitation, postural correction, and low-back pain. In fact, it does seem that fewer and fewer trainers seem to concentrate on simply getting people stronger and fitter, which is what the job is actually all about.

So, how do you go about finding someone? Getting results and training safely and effectively should be high on your priority list. The following is a list of some things you should consider and look for in a trainer before hiring them to work with you.

- Ask about their current clientele and if they can show you any testimonials, better still could you speak to some of their clients? A good trainer should be only too keen for you to do this, as their clients should be their best advert for what they do.
- Ask about their qualifications and get some information on how they can help you to achieve your goals. Ask for examples of how they have done this with previous clients.
- Ask about the last training course they went on, what was it and how long ago was it? If they tell you it was with the YMCA in 1996 then make your excuses and walk away.
- Make sure you are totally clear on cancellation policies, payment terms, and what the fees include. Most trainers offer discounts for block bookings paid in advance.
- Ask them to explain their assessment procedure. At the very minimum this should include some type of movement screening and postural assessment to accompany the more rudimentary health questions and blood pressure checks. If they do not assess you, then they simply cannot write a training programme that is anymore than guesswork. My advice is to steer well clear of any trainers who do not do this as a matter of course.
- Finally, remember that this is an investment in your health and training and therefore should be approached with the same care that you would take to buy a house or a new car. Take your time to see a few trainers and give thought to it before you put your money and your body in their hands.

PART **TWO**

UPPER BODY EXERCISES

4

Horizontal pushes

The bench press

The bench press is the lift by which all others seem to be judged. Yet for all its popularity many people frequently perform it with appalling technique. A few simple adjustments to your bench press technique will be reflected in improved strength and reduced rates of injury. One of the most common mistakes made during the many versions of this exercise is to position the feet up on the bench, often to relieve the stress on the lower back. Doing this creates instability and prevents the transfer of force through the body, in short reducing the amount you can lift. The simplest way to prevent this is to either use a lower bench, or to place a step at the end of the bench to put your feet on. You should also avoid flaring the elbows out excessively wide. Although sometimes recommended to focus the effort on the chest, what this actually does is greatly increase the stress on the shoulder without greatly improving the strength of the movement. Of course, everybody has slightly different lever lengths and biomechanics so it is always best to find an arm position that works best for you.

Barbell bench press

Muscle focus – chest, anterior shoulder, triceps

Exercise 1a	Barbell bench press

The barbell version of the bench press is probably the best-known exercise in the weights room and certainly one of the most commonly

Exercise 1b   Incline variation

- Lower the bar all the way to your chest under control. Bouncing the bar off your chest is cheating and potentially dangerous. By controlling the movement you will overload your chest more effectively.
- Explosively press the bar back to the start, keeping your back tight and your backside on the bench.
- Focus on driving the weight up as if you were pushing yourself into the bench. Drive your feet through, keeping your chest high and technique and form precise.

practised. It is best suited to improving maximal strength due to the heavier weights that can be used and the bilateral nature of the movement. For this reason it should ideally be performed with the aid of a spotter. To prevent overtraining it is best to add variety with dumbbells, different training speeds, and changes in movement. The incline and decline versions of the lift shown above are two examples, which change the motor recruitment patterns needed to perform the exercise.

- Set yourself up with your eyes directly under the bar and your feet planted firmly on the floor directly under your knees.
- There should be an arch in your back, though not an overarched lower back. To achieve this keep your chest lifted throughout the movement.
- Take a firm grip of the bar with your thumbs wrapped around it. Grip width is very individual with a wider grip reducing the work on the triceps. Somewhere around 2 feet apart is usually suitable.
- Stay tight through the shoulders with your shoulder blades retracted to create a stable base to press the weight against.

Dumbbell bench press

Muscle focus – chest, anterior shoulder, triceps

Exercise 2a	Dumbbell bench press

Exercise 2b	Stability ball variation

Exercise 2c	Alternate arms variation

The dumbbell versions of this lift provide far greater scope for variety than when performed with the barbell. They are also safer if you are training on your own as the weights can be dropped if absolutely necessary. Try the exercise using only one dumbbell or lowering one dumbbell while keeping the other in the lock-out position. Single limb exercise can also be used as a way to improve stability, a study by Behm et al in 2005 found greater levels of activation in the trunk muscles with a single arm chest press and back stabilisers with the overhead press, compared to the bilateral versions.

- Set up for this exercise as for the barbell version.
- Dumbbells are held in a pronated grip, although to reduce the stress on your shoulders a neutral grip can also be used with the palms facing each other (this is preferable for most trainees to reduce the possibility of shoulder injury and to allow for greater range of movement).
- Lower the dumbbells under control to your chest.
- Press the dumbbells back to the start position.

Close grip bench press

Muscle focus – triceps, anterior shoulder, chest

Exercise 3a	Close grip bench press

Exercise 3b	Incline variation

bigger and better arms. For variety it can also be done in an incline or decline position.

- Begin supine on the bench with your feet flat on the floor and your chest high.
- Take a grip on the bar with your hands slightly inside shoulder width.
- Lower the bar all the way to your chest, keeping your elbows close to your body.
- Press the bar explosively back upwards and slightly backwards to return to the start position.

The close grip press places a far greater emphasis on the triceps than its wider grip variant. It is an excellent assistance exercise to strengthen the arms and help build bench press performance and can also be performed in either an incline or decline position. It also allows heavier weights to be used than normal for a triceps exercise so it is an excellent movement for developing strength in the arms, in particular in the fast-twitch muscle fibres. This is a must-do movement for anyone wanting

T-Press-ups

Muscle focus – chest, anterior shoulder, triceps, core

Exercise 4	T-Press-ups

The press-up has for years been used as a test of upper body strength and endurance. This simple variation is one of many tweaks that can add a challenge to the well-known original movement. As well as strengthening the chest and arms, the T-press-up adds both a rotational and stability challenge to the exercise. Get more variety through altering the hands to an offset position.

- Begin in the press-up position with your hands at the same height as your shoulders.

Add dumbbells for a greater challenge.
- Position your feet slightly wider than for a normal press-up.
- As you push upwards rotate one arm towards the ceiling keeping your body in good alignment. Be sure not to let your hips drop and your lower back arch as you do this.
- Slowly return back to the start position and repeat on the opposite side.

Power press-ups

Muscle focus – chest, anterior shoulder, triceps, core

Exercise 5a	Power press-ups

Adding an explosive element to the press-up can help activate the fast-twitch muscle fibres that are key to producing fast, dynamic movement. A study by Vossen et al in 2000 of 38 women found the plyometric/power press-up performed from the knees to be more effective than a normal dynamic press-up in improving upper body strength. Try adding this exercise to your routine, particularly if you are involved in sports where upper body strength is important, such as rugby. For a more advanced version, you can try drop press-ups where you begin

Exercise 5b	Drop press-up variation

with both hands on boxes placed to each side and drop off to the floor, explosively pressing back up onto the boxes (see photo).

- Begin in the standard press-up position and ensure you maintain good alignment throughout the exercise.
- Lower towards the floor and explode back up pushing yourself away from the floor.
- Dynamically drop back into the bottom position of the press-up and explode upwards again using the momentum from the bottom of the movement.

Dips

Muscle focus – chest, anterior shoulder, triceps

Exercise 6	Dips

The dip has come in for its fair share of criticism lately for leading to shoulder problems. While this movement should not be at the top of your training sheet if you have a history of shoulder problems, it is still included in training programmes by many with great success for building pushing strength and impressive tricep definition. Varying grip and body position can change the emphasis of this exercise. A narrower grip coupled with a more upright position favours the triceps and the anterior deltoid of the shoulder. Taking a wider grip and leaning forwards more tends to accentuate the chest and more extreme variants of this (such as the Gironda dip) are popular in bodybuilding circles for improving pectoral definition and size.

- Start on the parallel bars with your arms just outside shoulder width apart.
- Keeping your abdominals braced, lower your body to the desired depth (this must **not** exceed the passive range of shoulder extension).
- Pushing the dip bar into the floor press back to the start position.

Stability ball press-up

Muscle focus – chest, triceps, shoulder stabilisers

Exercise 7	Stability ball press-up

The stability ball press up places far greater demand on the stabilising muscles of the shoulder and lower back/abdominals than it does on the movement muscles. This is a great exercise for improving dynamic shoulder stability and is surprisingly demanding. The inherently unstable nature of this exercise makes it all too easy to be done with poor form. It is a good idea to keep an eye on your form in the mirror to prevent your hips dropping or your upper back rounding, both compensations for a lack of abdominal strength. As with all exercises, once form starts to suffer you should stop and move on to the next exercise.

- Begin in the press-up position with your hands on a well-inflated stability ball. Pay close attention to the position of your hips and upper back. Your body should be optimally aligned from toe to head without excessive arch in the lower back or rounding in the upper back.
- Slowly lower your chest towards the ball, maintaining a strong position with the abdominals braced.
- Extend back to the start position.

Medicine ball chest pass

Muscle focus – chest, anterior shoulder, triceps, core

Exercise 8	Medicine ball chest pass

This drill is best performed with a partner or trainer but if you can't find anyone willing then a decent wall will do the job. By involving a catch and throw it can help develop reaction, coordination, and speed. You can also create further variety by passing one-handed, with or without rotation, or by adding in a squat or lunge to the throwing movement.

- Begin with the ball held in two hands close to your chest, either in a square or split stance.
- Throw the ball to your partner (or against your wall) as hard as it is safe to do so. Remember though to develop speed and power the intent should be to move the weight quickly!
- Keep your arms outstretched to form a target for the return pass.
- Catch the ball flexing at the elbow and shoulder to absorb the weight, quickly reversing the movement to return the ball back to your partner. Do not pause between catching and throwing the ball as you are trying to train reactive speed with this exercise.

Vertical pushes

Military press

Muscle focus – mid-shoulders, triceps

Exercise 9	Military press

The word military in this exercise is synonymous with the strict form that should be employed when performing it. A true military press is performed standing with a slightly

narrower stance than a regular press, and without any assistance from the lower body. While I can understand the necessity for strict form, the notion of performing this with the heels together, seems to make little sense. Lifting a heavy weight overhead with such a narrow base of support seems a slightly questionable practice. For that reason I recommend using a shoulder width stance for this exercise. The shoulders respond well to higher volumes, but vary between movements to prevent imbalances. Use drop sets, supersets, and pre/post fatigue for best results. Those with excellent shoulder mobility may choose to perform the behind neck version of this lift, although many will find the range of movement detrimental to good shoulder health.

- Begin with the barbell held across the front of your shoulders.
- Take a grip on the bar with your hands outside shoulder width.
- Keep your chin and chest up and your shoulders retracted.
- Keeping your body totally still the barbell is driven overhead to a locked-out position.
- The barbell should be in line with your ears when overhead.
- Lower under control to the start position.

Single arm overhead press (standing)

Muscle focus – shoulders, triceps

Exercise 10	Single arm overhead press

This is an excellent shoulder exercise suitable for just about anyone, as the single arm form with a neutral grip places minimal stress on the shoulder joint compared to other exercises. For lifting heavier weights, you can brace your body by using your spare arm to hold on to a convenient support.

- Start in a split stance with the same leg back as is holding the dumbbell.
- Hold the dumbbell at your shoulder with a neutral grip (palm facing inwards).
- Keep your chest up and eyes looking straight ahead.
- Keeping your abdominals braced, press the weight directly overhead to full extension of your arms. Your biceps should be in line with your ears.
- Lower the weight back to the start position carefully and under control.

Dumbbell push press

Muscle focus – shoulders, triceps

Exercise 11	Dumbbell push press

The push press could easily belong in the total body chapter of exercises as it really starts to involve everything from the floor upwards to press a weight overhead, allowing the hips and legs to help provide a driving force in order to complete each repetition. It is a useful exercise for developing overhead strength and power.

- Start with the dumbbells held at your shoulders in a neutral grip (palms facing inwards).
- Dip down into a quarter squat position flexing at the knees and ankles.
- As you extend up from the squat position press the weights explosively overhead.
- Lower the weights slowly back to the start position.

Arnold press

Muscle focus – mid and anterior shoulders, triceps

Exercise 12	Arnold press

This movement combines a rotation from the inwardly rotated start position to the external rotation and full shoulder flexion to finish. This exercise targets the shoulders, in particular the anterior deltoids. This movement does not really hold any great advantages over the regular shoulder press movement, but it does provide important variation for the nervous system and helps to keep stimulating adaptations.

- Begin with the dumbbells held at the front, with your palms facing into your chest.
- Raise the dumbbells overhead and as you do this, rotate your palms to face forwards.
- Lower the weights reversing the movement back to the start position.

Vertical pull

Dumbbell scaption

Muscle focus – anterior and mid-shoulder

Exercise 13	Dumbbell scaption

The scaption exercise is one of the more isolated exercises for the shoulders and is a better option for most people than the more common lateral raise as it allows the shoulder to work in a more natural plane of movement. The scaption is a great exercise to use as a pre/post fatigue movement in an upper body routine. To get the most from this movement, avoid the temptation to swing the weights up with upper body movement.

- Start with the dumbbells held either by your side or in front of your body.
- Raise both hands to an angle about 30 degrees from the frontal plane of your body.
- As you raise the weights, remember to keep your thumbs uppermost, as if trying to hitch a ride. This allows the upper arm to externally rotate as the shoulder flexes – a far more natural movement.
- Ensure that as you do this you are not

43

elevating the entire shoulder girdle; there should be no need to shrug your shoulders to complete this exercise.

- Raise the weights to just above shoulder height, lowering them slowly and under control.

Cuban press

Muscle focus – shoulders – external rotators, elevators, and deltoids

| Exercise 14 | Cuban press |

The original version of this lift was based on three distinct movements – a shrug, external rotation, and finally an overhead press. This movement can help strengthen the often-neglected external rotators of the shoulder (*infraspinatus* and *teres minor*) along with the scapula elevators. At first use dumbbells until you have fully mastered this movement.

- Begin by rowing the dumbbells up to your sternum with your upper arm held parallel to the ground and a right angle at the elbow. The palms of your hands will face backwards.
- Maintaining the upper arm position, rotate the dumbbells forwards until your forearm is vertical to the floor and palms are facing forwards.
- Resist the temptation to swing the weights or arch your back to get the weight up. If you need to do this then reduce the weights.

Chin-ups with variations

Muscle focus – lats, biceps

As a free weight and bodyweight exercise the chin-up (also known as a heave) has few rivals, both for building great strength and packing on some muscle in the upper back and arms. Remember, the body quickly adapts so to keep improving you should regularly change the grip position you use, forcing your body to recruit new muscle to perform it.

There are many, many different varieties of this exercise so to keep it simple we are going to cover the three main versions you can use to form the crux of your programme. Pull-ups are performed with the palms facing away and chin-ups with the palms facing towards you. If you find your grip or forearms fatiguing before your back then you can use straps around the bar for assistance. However, you should not become reliant on these, as grip strength should be improved along with everything else. To really develop arm strength and pulling power you must work through a full range and extend your arms fully at the end of each repetition.

You will feel and see far greater benefit in strength and muscular development if you do this.

Exercise 15a Wide grip pull-up

The wide grip version of this movement is perhaps the classic chin-up and the one used for tests in the military and other services all over the world. This version is great for developing the lats (*latissimus dorsi*, the large muscles that run the length of the back and form the distinctive V-shape of the upper body) as well as forearm and wrist strength.

- Begin with your hands spaced around 1.5 times shoulder width apart on the bar.
- Your arms should be fully extended and shoulders elevated.
- Pull up till your chin clears the bar keeping your feet crossed to help reduce swinging.
- As you pull up, fully depress your shoulder blades.
- Lower slowly under control back to full extension.

Exercise 15b Close grip chin-up

The close grip version of this exercise is performed with a supinated grip. In this position the palms are facing towards you and your hands are positioned narrower than shoulder width apart. This places far greater emphasis on the biceps that flex the elbow and is almost as much an arm exercise as it is anything else.

- Take a close grip on the bar with your hands 6–8 inches apart.
- Start from a fully extended position.
- Pull yourself up till your chin clears the bar.
- Slowly lower yourself back to the start position.

Exercise 15c Lean-away/sternal pull-up

This last version of the pull-up is a great way to combine the pulling movements of exercises such as the bent-over row, pullover, and chin-up together into one movement. Another one from the brain of Vince Gironda, this advanced chin-up variation will challenge even the strongest of lifters. If there is only one chin-up you can do then this is probably a good bet!

- Start as for a standard pull up with your arms fully extended and shoulders elevated.
- You can use a wide range of grips for this, it is best to start with a closer grip supinated version, while the more advanced lifter might use a wider pronated position.
- As you pull up lean away from the bar, bringing the bottom of your chest to touch the bar.
- Lower under control to the start position.

Upright pulls

Muscle focus – upper trapezius, biceps, shoulders

Exercise 16a   Upright pulls

The upright pull or clean pull is an excellent exercise to build strength for Olympic lifts, but is an exercise that again should be used with care

Exercise 16b   Dumbbell variation

by those with poor posture and rounded shoulders. To increase the crossover to Olympic lifting this movement can also be performed as a power pull where you pull the bar explosively upwards shrugging the shoulders and extending powerfully through the hips. This movement will allow you to shift far greater weight and sets a platform for moving to the hang power clean exercise. This version is different to the conventional upright row exercise in that the bar is not pulled up to underneath the chin, instead it is only pulled as high as the sternum. Lifting a weight all the way to the chin is pointless for many as it requires an extreme range of shoulder mobility and has questionable levels of crossover to sports or everyday life.

- Begin with the weights held in front of your body, palms facing towards you.
- The grip used can either be relatively narrow (shoulder width) or a wide grip. The wide grip involves the back to a greater degree and is an assistance movement for the snatch exercise. As less elbow flexion is possible with this, bar height will also be lower.
- Keep the weight close to your body and pull upwards as far as the sternum, there is little to be gained from going past this point.
- Lower under control to the start position.

Medicine ball football throws

Muscle focus – lats, abdominals

Exercise 17	Medicine ball football throws

This is another medicine ball movement that can either be performed on your own or with a partner. This is a great exercise for developing total body throwing power as it allows the whole kinetic chain to be involved in a natural and functional recruitment pattern. It is also an excellent movement for training the abdominals to work from a position of spinal extension to spinal flexion – both stabilising and controlling movement and generating power. Reversing this movement also provides an excellent dynamic exercise for building explosive upper body power, targeting the extensor muscles of the posterior chain. To do this, simply take the ball forwards into a flexed position to start the movement. From this position keep the arms long and extend the hips to propel the ball back overhead.

- Begin with the ball held at waist level, feet shoulder width apart and abdominals braced.
- Take the ball back overhead as if doing a throw-in at football or rugby. You should aim to achieve extension through your hips and upper back to do this. Use your abdominals to control this extension and ensure you are not simply arching your lower back.
- Keeping your arms long, explosively drive them forwards by using the strength of your abdominals and hip flexors.
- Aim for distance or power by throwing the ball to a partner or against a wall – a squash court is the perfect place to practice this.

Horizontal Pulls

Single arm bench row

Muscle focus – lats, shoulder retractors, biceps

Exercise 17	Single arm bench row

The single arm row using a bench is a basic beginner's exercise using the stable surface of the bench to support the body so that the trainee can focus on the pulling part of the movement. Despite its simplicity this exercise is often performed with terrible form – excessive rotation through the lumbar spine is potentially dangerous and should be avoided. This movement can provide a useful introduction to pulling movements for the novice lifter.

- Begin with one knee and the ipsilateral (same side) hand resting on a bench in a three-point stance.
- Your body should be in good alignment with a neutral spine position.
- Draw the dumbbell up towards your armpit, maintaining a neutral position at the lumbar spine but allowing your shoulder to move towards the ceiling and some rotation to happen in your upper back. This is natural and should not be prevented.
- Lower the weight under control to the start position.

Inverted rows

Muscle focus – biceps, shoulder retractors, lats

Exercise 18	Inverted rows

The inverted row is a fantastic bodyweight exercise that often highlights weakness in the retractors of the shoulders. This movement is the direct opposite of the bench press and really targets the muscles that often become weak with too much chest work. It is a very versatile bodyweight movement that is easily adaptable to allow for progression, making it suitable for novices or more advanced lifters. Try it single armed for an even greater challenge. You **must** use a securely anchored or racked barbell for this exercise.

- Begin with both hands pronated (palms down) on the barbell wider than shoulder width apart. To target the elbow flexors over the back you can supinate the hands and use a narrow grip.
- Start with your feet flat on the floor, knees bent and your body held in good alignment with your abdominals well braced.
- Drawing your shoulders back, pull your chest up to the bar.
- Fully extend back to the start position under control.
- To increase the challenge you can move your feet further away, or change the lever by placing them on a bench or stability ball.

Bent over row

Muscle focus – shoulder retractors, upper trapezius, biceps

Exercise 19	Bent over row

The bent over row has long been one of the staple strength training exercises in weight rooms everywhere. This exercise predominantly hits the upper back but also challenges the stabilising function of the mid-section, lower back, and hips to hold a steady and safe position while lifting a heavy weight. All too often as people fatigue on this movement it is the posture that is the first thing to falter. A variation as subtle as changing the grip from supinated to pronated can make a significant difference to the muscle recruitment patterns in this exercise. Alternatively, dumbbells can be used – allowing for alternate or single arm movement and therefore greater range of movement for the shoulder girdle. This exercise is also sometimes performed with the bar from the floor or blocks.

- Begin with your feet wider than shoulder width apart to create a stable base.
- You hands can be in a pronated or supinated grip. As before, the supinated position for the hands places the elbow flexors in a more advantageous position to assist with exercise.
- With the bar held with your arms fully extended, bend over from your hips with your knees also flexed. Ensure that you do not round your lower back at any point during the exercise.
- Keeping good alignment throughout your spine (including the cervical spine, where the tendency is for people to hyperextend), row the bar in to the mid-section.
- Slowly and under control extend your arms fully back to the start position.

Dumbbell pullovers

Muscle focus – lats, chest (*pectoralis minor* and *major*)

Exercise 20	Dumbbell pullovers

The pullover targets in particular the *pectoralis minor* – a muscle of the chest – as well as the *latissiumus* in the back, but for anyone with limited shoulder mobility or short and stiff abdominals this is probably not the wisest choice of exercise to perform with a heavy load. Done with a light load it can, however, help to improve the range of movement and thoracic extension as a corrective exercise. This movement requires excellent abdominal strength as, with a heavy weight, there is a high risk of abdominal tears or herniations.

- Begin with a dumbbell held over your chest with your arms extended.
- Keeping a slight bend in your arms, lower them directly overhead, keeping your abdominals well braced and ensuring your lower back does not arch.
- Only lower as far as your active range* of movement allows, before reversing the movement and returning to the start position.

*Active range means the range that you can move the joint through using only muscle action. Passive range is the range that you can move the joint through using either assistance from someone else or an implement such as a strap or dumbbell.

Single arm bent over row

Muscle focus – shoulder retractors, biceps, core

Exercise 21	Single arm bent over row

The dumbbell row is a nice variation on the more traditional bent-over row. However, because this movement does involve a strong rotational element, proper attention to form is essential to reduce the risk of injury to the lumbar spine. It is a great exercise for anyone involved in sports or occupations where single arm lifting is frequently involved, such as firefighters or builders.

- Begin in the bent over position used for the barbell bent over row exercise.
- Row the dumbbell in towards your armpit, allowing the thoracic spine to rotate and the shoulder girdle to move backwards to a greater degree than is possible with the barbell version.
- Great care must be taken not to rotate through the lumbar spine during this exercise.
- The movement should be controlled at all times and should be immediately stopped upon fatigue (normally the postural stabilisers).

Strengthening the shoulder

Good shoulder function is directly related to the ability of the shoulder muscles to keep the head of the humerus in the right place during movement and if you overhead lift regularly or are in a sport where pressing movements predominate, then adding some simple exercises to your programme can help to minimise the chance of imbalances developing. Balance push movements with pulls (protraction with retraction) and presses with vertical pulls (elevation with depression) and internal rotation with external. If you sit at a desk most of the day, then use a 2:1 ratio of rowing to pressing movements and take care with shoulder work, favouring pulling and external rotation patterns over all others.

Try these three exercises to protect those easily weakened muscles of the shoulder that are commonly neglected in most weight rooms, leading to many shoulder problems. These exercises work best using 8–12 repetitions and 3–4 sets. If you find you are especially weak in these movements, perform them at the start of your workout.

Seated external rotation

Exercise 22	Seated external rotation

This exercise is a basic movement to strengthen the external shoulder rotators (*infraspinatus* and *teres minor*) that are often neglected in a conventional strength training programme and is a must for anyone who bench presses or does a lot of chin-ups. Ensure you work through the full range of movement, controlling the eccentric phase in particular.

- To begin, sit on a bench with one leg on the bench, foot flat and knee flexed.
- Keeping your torso upright and facing forwards, place your elbow on the inside of your knee, a couple of inches lower than your shoulder.
- Your forearm should be directly vertical to the floor.
- Lower the weight slowly, then pause before returning to the start position.

Trap lifts single arm

Press-up plus

Exercise 23	Trap lifts single arm

Exercise 24	Press-up plus

The trap lift targets another upward rotator – the lower trapezius – commonly found wanting in many people. The key to this exercise is to focus on scapula movement, ensuring you don't shrug the shoulders up as you lift the weight, instead concentrating on maintaining the retracted and depressed position.

- Use a bench inclined to around 45 degrees for this exercise, with your forehead resting on the end. Ensure you have a neutral spine position.
- Begin by allowing your arm to hang fully extended with a light weight. Start light and work on control and form before increasing.
- Retract and depress your shoulder blade.
- Raise your arm upwards and to the side.
- Raise until your arm is in line with your ear without elevating your shoulder.

This exercise is designed to strengthen a muscle called the *serratus anterior*. The serratus has an important job to do in rotating the shoulder blade upwards during movement. This exercise has been shown to be highly effective (along with scaption movements) in improving *serratus* function.

- Begin in a normal press up position with good body alignment
- Keeping your body in line, allow gravity to take the shoulders, letting your shoulder blades retract and your chest drop towards

the floor. Keep your abdominals working when you do this to maintain alignment.

- Press back through the shoulder girdle, rounding your shoulders, all the time maintaining good form through the spine. Aim to keep your shoulder blade tight to the ribcage.

Assistance exercises

Assistance movements in this case refer to exercises that target either the elbow flexors or the elbow extensors. Training for the arms forms a valid and in some cases important part of training, not to mention it is good fun at the end of a tough workout. Granted, if you only train once a week, then work for the biceps may not be high on your priority list, but for anyone weight training regularly, aiming to build their bigger lifts, bodybuilding, training for aesthetics, or involved in activities where arm and grip strength are important then it is an important part of a training approach. Next follow some movements for each muscle group, along with some ideas to create further variety in your arm routine.

Scott curls (preacher curls)

Assistance focus – elbow flexors (biceps)

| Exercise 25 | Scott curls |

Named after Mr Olympia – Larry Scott – this exercise prevents cheating by fixing the elbows in place. Using the EZ bar places the hands in a slightly more pronated position, slightly taking the load from the biceps brachii and sharing it with the brachialis.

Despite the idea of this exercise being to isolate and fatigue the biceps, people often contort themselves into terrible positions to squeeze out extra reps. This is completely unnecessary, once you can no longer complete a curl with perfect form the set is complete. If you haven't got a preacher bench to hand, simply incline a normal bench and rest the elbow on the pad. You can also perform versions such as the Zottman curl using this bench.

- You should be seated at the bench so that your forearms can rest on the pad at full extension without any distress to the elbow joint.
- Take the bar while standing and then sit in place.

- Begin with your forearms fully extended, chin up throughout the whole movement.
- Curl the bar up until your forearms are vertical to the floor.
- Keep your chin and chest up throughout the movement to maximally stress the biceps.
- Lower the weight slowly and under control back to a position of full extension at your elbow joint.

Zottman curls

Muscle focus – elbow flexors and forearms

Exercise 26	Zottman curls

This tweak on the normal arm curl stresses the biceps and *brachioradialis*, building both the upper and lower arms. The weaker position on the lowering phase means you will probably use a slightly lower weight than for standard arm curls. To get the most from this exercise ensure you keep your body totally still and really concentrate on lowering the weight under control. You can also perform this using a preacher bench.
- Begin by standing with your arms fully extended and your palms facing forwards.

- Curl the dumbbells up to your shoulders, keeping your body perfectly still and elbows close in to your sides.
- At the top of the movement, rotate your wrists so that the palms of your hands face away from you.
- Lower the weight from this position slowly under control.

Standing straight bar curls

Muscle focus – elbow flexors – biceps

Exercise 27	Standing straight bar curls

The straight bar curl is still regarded as the most effective single biceps movement you can do, although as we have already seen, variety is the most important key in keeping exercises effective. There really isn't much more to this than simply keeping good form and concentrating on getting maximum tension in those biceps.
- Begin by standing with your elbows into your sides and body in good alignment.
- From a position of full extension, flex your elbow and curl the weight up to the top position.
- Lower the weight slowly under control.

Reverse curls

Muscle focus – elbow flexors – brachialis

Exercise 28	Reverse curls

Underneath the main biceps heads is a muscle called the *brachialis*, the main elbow flexor when the hand is pronated (palm down). This is because the biceps have a far weaker line of pull in this position so you will probably be using a weight around 75% of what you would use for a conventional arm curl with the palms supinated.

Strengthening the brachialis will increase your arm strength overall and is particularly useful for improving pull-up ability where the hands are in a pronated position on the bar.

- Begin with your arms fully extended and the bar held with your palms facing inwards.
- Keeping your elbows and your body still, curl the weight up to your shoulders.
- Avoid curling your wrists into extension. Keep them in a neutral position to keep the focus on the brachialis.
- Lower the weight slowly to the start position.

Incline hammer curls

Muscle focus – elbow flexors – brachialis

Exercise 29	Incline hammer curls

Incline hammer curls place the emphasis squarely on the *brachialis* muscle in favour of the more commonly trained biceps. This is invaluable strengthening for any pulling movement performed with a neutral grip (palms facing each other). The incline position puts the elbows well behind the body, putting a lot of extra work on the biceps tendon, so take care if you have shoulder problems.

- Begin on an inclined bench with it set at around 45 degrees of incline.
- Your arms should be fully extended with your palms facing towards each other.
- Keeping your elbows fixed and palms facing each other, curl the weights up to your shoulder.
- Lower the weight slowly and under control.

French press

Muscle focus – elbow extensors – triceps

Exercise 30	French press

- Begin supine on a bench with your arms extended directly overhead, making sure you have enough room to lower the bar to your head without hitting the rack.
- Keeping your elbows fixed in place, slowly bend your arms, lowering the weight to your forehead/bridge of the nose area.
- From this position, extend your arms back to the start position.

Overhead triceps extension

Muscle focus – elbow extensors – triceps

Exercise 31	Overhead triceps extension

The French press, also known as a skullcrusher or nosebreaker, is another highly popular and effective arm exercise – a supine triceps extension. Keeping with the theme of creating as much variety as possible to your arm routines, try this exercise on the decline bench. From this position it will maximally stress each head of the triceps muscle. If you are new to lifting then it is wise to begin with dumbbells and progress onto the barbell or EZ bar when confident.

The overhead extension is a great exercise for hitting the whole of the triceps muscle and can be done in several formats – with a dumbbell, EZ bar, tricep bar, or even a straight bar. It can also be done from a range of positions such as seated (supported or unsupported), kneeling or standing.

- Start seated on the bench with your back fully supported.
- Lower the weight slowly behind your head.
- Keep your upper arm vertical and ensure that your back is not arched.

- Fixing your elbows, extend your arms to just short of lockout.
- Slowly lower the weight.

Grip strength

Improving grip strength is an often-overlooked aspect of training, yet is of particular value to a wide range of sports and activities. A weak grip can also become a limiting factor to using heavier weights in exercises such as deadlifts, chin-ups or bent-over rows where the forearms often fatigue early in the workout limiting the amount that can be done on later exercises. One solution is to use straps, which is fine for a bodybuilder but which for anyone else really isn't a solution to the actual problem. Grip strength is a key constituent for many sports such as climbing, horse riding, mixed martial arts, judo, rugby, and many occupations where getting and keeping hold of something, or someone, is important. Grip strength itself is also usually a good indicator of someone's overall strength, as people who tend to grip poorly probably are not very strong, whereas those with a strong grip often have the potential for greater strength.

Below are several different ways to improve grip strength.

Dedicated grip trainers

A popular choice for improving grip are the sprung-loaded implements that you can sit and squeeze repeatedly. They are normally very simple pieces of kit that consist of two handles joined by a loaded spring that is compressed to close the handles. Simple but reasonably effective these can be used throughout the day to build strength in the finger flexors. Their only disadvantage is that people tend to squeeze for repetitions, which is different to trying to hold onto an object against gravity as we shall see below.

Thick/oversize bars

The most common barbells are the standard Olympic style. However, there are other types of barbell that can be used as a great training tool for improving grip strength while having to apply force to something.

The added thickness of a 3-inch bar, for example, greatly increases the challenge on the muscles of the hand, wrist, and forearm. It forces you to concentrate harder on simply keeping hold of the bar and can save you time doing additional grip work as you get to improve it at the same time as doing your regular weights routine.

You can improvise by using something like foam lagging taped to a bar, dumbbells, or chin-up bars. Be careful the first time you do this, particularly if lifting overhead as you may drop the bar. For that reason it is advisable to have a spotter close at hand and to do the exercise in a power rack with safety stops in place.

Using towels, ropes, tennis balls and weight plates

Taking our improvised training a step further, you can use something like a towel or rope to try to grip instead of the actual weight. For example, try knotting a towel around a heavy dumbbell and see how far you can walk while keeping hold of the weight – not too easy is it?

You could also try doing your chin-ups using a towel or rope to hold onto instead of the chin-up bars. This type of training will build the kind of strength needed to perform the elusive one-handed chin-up. Alternatively, simply try doing exercises like the scaptions for the shoulders holding onto a pair of weight plates instead of dumbbells.

Another option, instead of the specific grip strength trainer, is simply to squeeze a tennis ball for repetitions. This low-cost option can be used regularly as a simple supplementary exercise.

String and a broom handle

This is a popular exercise amongst rowers, who tend to have a pretty good grip anyway. Guaranteed to induce unpleasant sensations throughout the whole body, this is a simple but harshly effective method of training the wrist extensors, invaluable for any activity where you might use a pronated grip in particular.

You can make your own set-up using a weight plate, some string and a broom handle. Simply tie the weight plate to the broom handle using around 5 feet of string. To perform the exercise simply hold your arms out to the front with the broom handle held parallel to the floor. Rotate the handle towards you, gradually winding the string around it and raising the weight. Lower it under control and repeat to total fatigue for a great way to truly finish your workout and to feel like you have forearms like Popeye!

Strongman-type training

Strongman style training is making a serious comeback into more mainstream fitness and strength training. Exercises such as sled dragging, farmers' walks (walking while carrying two very heavy objects – typically something like an anvil), carrying or lifting awkward-shaped implements are now being used more in the conditioning of athletes.

These types of exercises build phenomenal grip strength and one reason is the tremendous variety of grip needed, along with an emphasis on developing total strength over muscle. Strongmen and women understand that being able to express strength is the key to succeeding in their lifts.

If you are keen to apply some strongman-type techniques to your training then it is relatively simple to begin. Try your own farmers' walk by using two heavy dumbbells and seeing

how far you can walk while holding them (*see* photo). A simple improvised version of this would be to fill two buckets with stones or to carry an awkward object (such as a patio slab or sandbag) and do the same thing.

Alternatively, try substituting your typical dumbbells for a more awkward shaped object when doing an exercise.

When training grip or lifting heavy weights, it is a good idea to get hold of some chalk to keep your hands dry. This is recommended rather than the use of gloves, which simply adds another layer that can slip and impair grip. It is also a good idea to wear something solid on your feet if grip training, as dropping a heavy weight on your toes is going to put the brakes on lifting for a few weeks! Whatever you do for building grip, use a variety of methods, particularly if you are in a sport where grip strength can make a significant difference to your ability to apply your wider strength. For example, great pulling power is useless in judo without the ability to exert it against a well-starched judo gi, a real exercise in grip strength and endurance.

Summary

There are many other upper body exercises possible using a variation on those mentioned above. Remember, something as simple as changing your grip position or stance can be enough to create a different challenge to the nervous system and keep the exercise effective. The upper body is neurally far more efficient than the lower body, meaning that it adapts to exercises faster and as such requires more regular changes to keep it stimulated.

LOWER BODY EXERCISES

5

Lower body movements are essential for any balanced free-weight training programme. They form the crux of athletic training routines, sports conditioning programmes, powerlifting, and bodybuilding approaches. They also have a central role in improving functional ability and activities of everyday living that are so important to everybody.

The squat

The squat is a knee dominant exercise that primarily targets the quadriceps muscles at the front of the thigh. A demanding exercise, it has long been the staple part of strength training regimes across the world and the subject of much study and discussion. There are many varieties of squat shown in the coming pages, but regardless of what version of the movement you use, the basic focus remains the same. Unfortunately, there are also many false truths surrounding this exercise that lead to erroneous guidelines being given so let's first deal with some of the common misunderstandings and grey areas that surround it.

The squat itself is one of the best core exercises you can do. There really is no substitute for 'real' strength that is developed through movements such as the squat and deadlift. These exercises simply cannot be performed successfully without adequate stability and mobility at the hips and mid-section.

How deep to squat is a subject of great debate. Most of the concern over squatting depth came from a study in the early 1960s that found ligaments in the knees of weightlifters to have been stretched as a result of deep (to the point where the hamstrings touch the calf muscles at the back of the leg) squatting. However, this study was later repeated with contradictory results and many weightlifters the world over full squat without terrible knee injuries. The squat is no different to any other exercise in that it should be performed through a full and pain free range of movement wherever possible. Unfortunately too many people succumb to the temptation to compromise squat depth to increase the weight lifted. If you cannot squat with the hips to a point below, or at least in line with the knees, with good form, then you should devote more work to mobility and exercises such as the split stance squat and toe touch squat, shown here, before you start adding more weight onto your squat bar. Similarly if you cannot squat maintaining good alignment of the ankle, knee and hip then you should spend time strengthening specific areas using exercises like the Petersen step up and split squat. Of course, for some people with mobility problems or functional limitations through illness or injury this won't always be possible. They should seek the advice of a well-qualified trainer on the version of the movement best suited for them.

Squats have been shown repeatedly in studies to be beneficial for knee stability and should form a core part of any strength training programme.

I am often asked about the practice of placing a lift under the heels to allow trainees to squat lower during a squat. This once popular pursuit is seen less today, but is not necessarily a bad thing, if done for the right reasons.

An inability to squat with adequate depth is usually a sign of poor flexibility. Placing a lift under the heels alters the available range of motion at the ankle joint and also shifts the centre of gravity forwards (see photo). This change in COG permits a more upright posture, while the opening of the ankle joint allows greater range of movement. There are often profound changes in squat performance when a heel lift is added. However, it should not be viewed as a long-term solution as it only treats the symptoms and not the actual problem. Dedicated mobility exercises, such as the overhead squat and the toe touch squat, should be performed along with stretching of tight areas and strengthening work for the posterior chain. These should be combined with a gradual reduction in the height of heel lift until you can perform a full range of movement without help.

The development of a full and correct pattern of movement in the squat should be the prime focus, prior to adding increased load to the movement.

Back squat

Muscle focus – quadriceps, glutes, hamstrings, lumbar erectors

Exercise 1a	Back squat

The back squat is one of the first movements novices to exercise are taught. It is the most practised of all the various squat movements and it has a wide range of applications. At greater depths the back squat actively involves the glutes and hamstrings to assist in extending the trunk back to the start position. It is also the version of the squat that allows the greatest weight to be lifted, which may explain its popularity amongst gym users. However, this also makes it the movement of choice for powerlifting.

Exercise 1b	Incorrect action – lumbar rounding

Exercise 1c	Incorrect action – excessive forward lean

- The bar should be positioned across the upper back and shoulder muscles* with your elbows directly underneath the bar.
- Position your feet at a comfortable distance apart, most lifters prefer a stance outside shoulder width with the feet slightly turned out and the weight more towards the heels.
- Keep your chest up, shoulders tight and look ahead during the movement.
- Sit back allowing your hips, knees, and ankles to flex.

- Your knees should move forward during this exercise to a point roughly over your toes, although this will differ between individuals. This will prevent excessive trunk lean and lower back injuries.
- Squat as deep as you can maintain form without rounding the lumbar spine. You may need someone to help you judge where this point is. Aim to maintain a good arch in the lower back.
- Extend back to the start position by driving your knees forwards and upwards, keeping your chest lifted.

During a full depth squat to a point of maximal knee flexion, the lumbar spine will not maintain a full lordotic (arched) position. This is simply a physical impossibility for all but the most gifted of people. However, if this happens at the bottom of the lift it is perfectly natural. It should not, however, occur earlier in the movement where the bar position can place undesirable torque forces on the lower back. If it does, more work should be devoted to hip mobility and strengthening of the spinal extensors.

* The Olympic style of squatting has a bar position higher on the shoulders in comparison to the powerlifting style that uses a much lower bar position and greater trunk lean. Use whichever you find most comfortable or best suited to your goals.

Overhead squat

Muscle focus – quadriceps, thoracic extensors

Exercise 2	Overhead squat

before progressing to a barbell. This exercise is a pre-requisite for performing the snatch.

- Start with your feet positioned slightly wider than shoulder width apart.
- Extend your arms overhead, locking out the elbow joint and keeping the palms of your hands facing forwards.
- Bending at the knee, hip, and ankle squat down and back without letting your arms fall forward.
- Squat to a depth where you can maintain good form. If you find it hard to achieve any sort of depth on this then start by raising your heels slightly using a rolled up towel or small weight plates or by performing the toe touch squat shown later.
- Extend back to the start position.
- Increase load using either dumbbells or barbell.

You **must** be able to overhead squat with good form before attempting Olympic lifts such as the snatch or jerk.

This versatile and challenging exercise can be used to develop mobility, stability and strength through the squat pattern of movement. It is advisable to begin this exercise unloaded and only start to introduce load to the movement once you can squat to parallel while maintaining the arms held straight overhead. It can also be performed in a single arm variation that allows for more trunk rotation. Start by using a wooden dowel or broomstick held overhead

Front squat

Muscle focus – quadriceps

Exercise 3a	Front squat

Exercise 3b	Zercher squat

Exercise 3c	Lifting straps

The front squat is seen a lot less in most weights room than the back squat, but among serious lifters it is a regular in their training routines. The front squat has some great benefits and forms an ideal training for the Olympic movements using a more erect trunk posture than the back squat. However, it is also an excellent exercise for targeting the quadriceps by reducing the involvement of the hip extensors. Many people find the hand position stressful on the wrists due to a lack of flexibility. You can get around this by simply using a pair of lifting straps wrapped around the barbell. Some lifters prefer to cross their arms with the thumbs under the bar – use whichever method you find most comfortable.

- Start with the barbell held across your shoulders. The bar should be resting on the deltoids (shoulder muscles) not your arms.
- Hold the bar with your fingers underneath and your wrists in extension. Your elbows should be driven forward and held high (see photo).

- Keeping your torso as upright as possible, flex through the hips, knees, and ankle to the desired depth while maintaining good form.
- Extend back to the start position.

A Zercher squat is a variety of the front squat, where the barbell is held in the crook of the elbows, keeping the torso upright.

Split stance squat (normal)

Muscle focus – quadriceps, glutes, adductors, hip stabilisers

Exercise 4	Split stance squat

If you have mobility problems in the full back or front squat, this is the ideal exercise to begin with. Progress by starting with your front foot elevated approximately 6–12 inches and focus on achieving a complete range of movement at the knee joint, allowing the knee to move past the toes and the hamstrings to touch the calf at the end of the movement. This movement builds excellent unilateral strength and helps develop the flexibility and strength needed to full squat. Once you can perform it successfully with the front foot elevated, move to a version with both feet on the floor and then finally to the Bulgarian version shown overleaf. Beginners should start this lift using dumbbells.

- Start in a large split stance with your front foot raised.
- Keep looking ahead and keep your chest raised throughout the movement.
- Drive your front knee forwards, keeping your heel fixed, until the hamstrings touch your calf.
- Extend your knee back to the start position and repeat.

Bulgarian split squat

Muscle focus – quadriceps, adductors, hip stabilisers

Exercise 5	Bulgarian split squat

in your lower back, simply raise the heel of the front foot using a towel or weight plate.
- Squat till your rear knee is just off the floor.
- Keep looking ahead and ensure that your shoulders are relaxed.
- Extend back to the start position.

The Bulgarian split squat is an excellent dumbbell or barbell exercise for the muscles of the thigh. Placing the rear foot in an elevated position focuses the effort on the front leg making this an ideal choice for home training or bodyweight routines.
- Start in a split stance with your rear foot elevated to around 18 inches–2 feet.
- Keep your trunk upright, dumbbells (if used) should be held by the side. If you cannot perform the exercise without hyper-extending

Single leg squat

Muscle focus – quadriceps, hip stabilisers

Exercise 6a	Single leg squat

Exercise 6b	Advanced single leg squat

The single leg squat is a great exercise for developing stability, strength, and balance, particularly for anyone who suffers from lower back problems and needs to overload the legs without subjecting the spine to increased compressive loading. As well as challenging the quadriceps, this movement places great emphasis on the stabilising muscles of the hip (*glute medius*, *minimus*, and *maximus*) which are often found wanting in many people.

Basic version
- Start by standing on one foot with the other leg slightly bent.
- Perform the squat movement, keeping your chest up and an arch in your lower back.
- Allow your knee to move forwards over your toes.
- Maintain good alignment of the hip, knee, and ankle.
- Keep the non-stance leg positioned next to the stance leg.
- Extend back to the start position.

Advanced version
- Stand on a box or bench.
- Extend the non-stance leg out to the front.
- Squat keeping your knee in alignment with your hip and ankle.
- Squat as deep as possible with good form.
- Extend back to the start position.

Jump squats

Muscle focus – quadriceps

Exercise 7a	Jump squats

Exercise 7b	Medicine ball variation

They can be performed with bodyweight, weight vest, medicine ball, or up to around 60% of bodyweight as resistance in the form of a barbell or dumbbells. They make an excellent metabolic workout when added to a circuit or can be used as a stand-alone exercise where the focus is on moving as quickly as possible.

- Begin in a standard squat stance, most suited to the specific requirements. Generally this is slightly wider than shoulder width.
- Drop into the squat position, ensuring you maintain good alignment of the ankle, knee, and hip.
- Without pausing at the bottom, explode back upwards into a vertical jump.
- Land with soft feet flexing through the joints to absorb the impact.

Jump squats are used to develop explosive strength and target the stretch-shortening actions of the muscle. This is a great exercise for improving the neural ability of the body to coordinate a dynamic effort.

Toe touch squat

Muscle focus – squat pattern development

Exercise 8	Toe touch squat

- Begin with your heels raised, either with towels, weight plates (see photo), or foam wedges.
- Reach overhead, keeping your abdominals tight and your ribcage pulled down.
- Perform a forward bend movement to touch your hands on the floor. Feel for the stretch in your hamstrings as you do this.
- Drop your hips towards the floor into a deep squat as far as possible.
- Reach overhead with both hands, making your spine long and lifting your chest.
- Extend through your hips to return to the start position, without rounding your upper back. Stay tall in the spine and keep your hands overhead.

The toe touch squat forms the basis for training an effective squat pattern through a full range of motion. This is one of the most effective exercises that beginners can use to develop a sound base of movement in the squat exercise, or as an active warm up movement. If you find it hard to squat to a depth where the thighs are at least parallel to the floor with good form, then this exercise is a great choice to improve range.

Lifts

The deadlift

Exercise 9	Alternate grip

As an exercise the deadlift has never been as popular as the squat among the recreational lifter, yet it is perhaps the most brutal expression of strength to be seen in a gym. So called because the bar starts from a 'dead' position on the floor for each repetition, it is a tough lift that can bring great rewards. It is the exercise at which it is possible to lift the greatest amount of weight and therefore it is a fundamental movement for powerlifting. However, its application moves well beyond powerlifting into many different uses as it targets such a fundamental pattern of movement. The deadlift is also an excellent training movement for the Olympic lifts as they too all begin from the floor (except for the hang versions).

In contrast to the squat, the deadlift primarily targets the hip extensors – *gluteus maximus*, hamstrings, and spinal erectors. Although the quadriceps are involved to extend the knee, their contribution is relatively small by comparison. The deadlift will also build a strong grip and it is often maintaining a grip on the bar that novice lifters find to be one of the hardest aspects of this lift. There are a number of grip options and the lift is usually taught initially with the use of a double overhand grip. However, some lifters prefer to use the alternate grip where one hand holds the bar in a supinated position (see photo).

Barbell deadlift

Muscle focus – glutes, hamstrings, back

Exercise 10a	Barbell deadlift

Exercise 10b   Dumbbell variation

The most basic variation of the deadlift is also the toughest and biggest lift in the gym and an excellent raw expression of strength. An excellent training movement for the Olympic lifts it is also a great exercise for strengthening the hamstrings, hips, lower and upper back. You can also add a multi-planar emphasis to the deadlift by reaching down towards one side or the other using dumbbells. This movement is ideal training for anyone in a job where they have to lift and carry things.

- Take a stance around shoulder width or slightly wider with the bar 2–4 inches from your shins.
- Take a grip on the bar with your hands positioned wide enough to be able to clear your knees and shins as you lift the bar. Your arms should be locked out straight.
- Keeping your lower back arched, chest high, and looking ahead you are ready to begin the lift.
- Initially focusing on pulling the bar up and back, drive your knees back, thrusting your hips forwards and upwards until you are in the finish position. Take care not to hyper-extend your lower back at the end of the lift.
- Reverse the movement by returning the bar to the floor.

If flexibility does not permit a full range of movement, you can begin and end the lift on blocks. Although due effort should be given to identifying any limitations to movement and rectifying them. The hamstrings are a common cause of this problem.

Single leg deadlifts

Muscle focus – glutes, hip stabilisers

Exercise 11	Single leg deadlifts

The single leg deadlift is a great alternative to the barbell versions of this exercise and is one of the best exercises for developing single leg stability. Performing the movement on one foot requires far greater involvement of the hip abductors to stabilise the body and maintain balance. To get maximum involvement from the muscles of the backside (gluteals) as opposed to purely hamstrings, ensure that you perform this exercise with a bend at the knee of around 20 degrees.

- Begin on one leg with the dumbbell held in the opposite hand to the stance leg.
- Ensure that you keep an arch in your lower back throughout the exercise.
- Bend forward from your hips, **not** from your lower back. Keep your chest high and resist the urge to flex through the upper spine.
- Allow your knee to bend and keep the arm holding the weight long.
- Return to the start position, reset (touching the foot down if necessary) and repeat.

Romanian deadlift (RDL)

Muscle focus – hamstrings, lower back

Exercise 12	Romanian deadlifts

This is a straight leg deadlift exercise that starts from the finish position of a regular deadlift.

The RDL helps to train the position known as the hang that is used in exercises such as the hang clean and the hang snatch as well as training the hamstrings in their role as hip extensors.

- Begin with the bar held in the hang position with your arms straight gripping the bar at around shoulder width or slightly wider.
- Unlock your knees and using **only** the hips lower the bar towards your knees. The knees should **not** move forwards during this movement and your ribcage is effectively locked onto the pelvis.
- Your hips will sway back allowing the bar to remain in contact with your thigh throughout the movement.
- Lower the bar to just above your knees.
- Extend through your hips back to the start position.

Good morning

Muscle focus – hamstrings, lower back, glutes

Exercise 13	Good morning

This is in my opinion a really underused exercise, often through misunderstanding and poor technical performance. Done correctly it strengthens the entire posterior chain of the body and will help to develop the forward bending motion while emphasising use of the hips for trunk extension. It is an excellent choice of strengthening exercise to improve squat and deadlift performance.

- Begin with the barbell supported across your shoulder in a similar position to that for a back squat.
- Unlock your knees and hinge forward from the hips, keeping your chest up (to prevent the lumbar spine flexing).
- Focus on keeping the abdominals braced to maintain an arch in your lower back.
- Only go forward as far as hamstring flexibility allows, without the lumbar spine flexing.
- Extend through your hips back to the start position.

Lunges and steps

Lunging/stepping

Lunge and stepping patterns make for some great exercises, their dynamic nature and integrated movement means that they can be used to offer a metabolic challenge as easily as they can build stability or strength.

For a functional movement, both of these movements help to replicate muscle recruitment patterns that are shared by gait, meaning that they can help strengthen and build unilateral (asymmetric) stability and balance – essential for both sports activities and common everyday movements.

The lunge movement targets the muscles of the hips and the legs so it is an excellent structural exercise for those keen to improve muscle definition in the lower extremity.

Barbell dynamic lunge

Muscle focus – quadriceps, glutes

Exercise 14a	Barbell dynamic lunge

Exercise 14b	Medicine ball variation

Exercise 14c	Kettlebell variation

The dynamic lunge can be performed with a barbell for greater loads or just as easily with dumbbells (great for building grip strength and working the forearms) and is a great exercise for developing total body stability as well as strength and power in the legs and hips. This dynamic movement also helps develop great stability in all three planes of movement forcing the core to work hard to maintain a strong body position and alignment. Begin with bodyweight and progress to dumbbells then barbells.

- Start with your feet shoulder width apart with the weight either positioned across your shoulders (if using a barbell) or held at your side (when using dumbbells).
- Take a large stride forwards keeping both feet pointing straight ahead and the trunk erect.
- Allow your knee to travel forwards and lower your hips towards the floor.
- Ensure that your knee stays in line with your hip and foot. Do **not** allow it to cave inwards.

Lower to a point where the rear knee is just off the floor.
• Keeping your trunk erect press off the mid-foot back to the start position.

Overhead lunge

Muscle focus – quadriceps, glutes, core

Exercise 15	Overhead lunge

Similar to the overhead squat, the lunge version challenges the whole body from top to toe. This movement won't overload the legs or hips to the extent that the previous version will, but it will build superb balance, mobility, and stability. You can use a variety of different types of resistance for this exercise, such as a barbell, dumbbells, powerbag or weight plate. You can also perform a single arm version that is slightly less demanding or perform walking lunges for a greater challenge.
• Start with your feet shoulder width apart holding a weight overhead with your arms fully extended.
• Stride forwards as for the dynamic lunge, keeping your arms locked out directly overhead.
• Maintaining good alignment throughout your body, stride back to the start position.

Lateral lunge

Muscle focus – quadriceps, adductors, hip stabilisers

Exercise 16	Lateral lunge

The lateral lunge helps build strength and stability in the less commonly trained frontal plane of movement. This is a common movement in sports like tennis where movement is through all three planes of motion. Combine this movement with other exercises such as an arm curl or shoulder press to make a more challenging whole body exercise. For improving dynamic power you can add in a medicine ball throw to the lunge movement.
• Start with your feet shoulder width apart, dumbbells (if used) can be held at the side.
• Take a large stride out to the side, keeping your torso upright and your hips facing forwards.
• Bend at the ankle, knee, and hip, lowering onto the stance leg, keeping good alignment throughout the movement.
• Descend as far as possible while maintaining good form.
• Extend through your hips and legs back to the start position and repeat to the other side.

Multi-plane lunge

Muscle focus – quadriceps, glutes, hip stabilisers, core

Exercise 17	Multi-plane lunge

Step ups (forward and lateral)

Muscle focus – quadriceps, glutes

Exercise 18a	Forward step ups

The multi-plane lunge introduces the use of the lunge movement through multiple directions and planes of motion, which is ideal when training for activities that involve direction changes, such as football, rugby, or squash. The version shown below is combined with a reaching movement but it can just as easily be used with a curl, press, or rotation.

- Begin with the basic reaching lunge forwards and repeat on each leg.
- Move next to the lateral lunge, performing one on each leg.
- Finally add a transverse plane variation, stepping the lead leg diagonally backwards.
- Imagine you are standing at the centre of a clock face, first lunge to 12, then to 3/9 then to 5/7.

Exercise 18b	Lateral step ups

Exercise 18c	Lateral step up starting position

As with squatting, the greater the amount of hip flexion used will involve the hip extensors to a larger extent. To encourage greater hip flexion, simply use a higher step.

Step ups are great exercises for strengthening the quadriceps (the muscles at the front of the thigh). They often form an early-stage rehabilitation exercise for people with knee or hip problems as they can be easily progressed from comparatively easy to very challenging. The step up is also excellent as it requires stability from the hip and core to maintain good body alignment from the foot to the head.

- For forward step ups, begin by standing behind the step, facing towards it. For the lateral version, start standing behind the step but facing at a right angle to it (see photo).
- Place the stance leg onto the step ensuring that your foot, knee, and hip all remain in good alignment.
- Step up, maintaining good alignment and keeping your trunk upright. A common mistake is to lean forward at the hip, a compensation for weak quadriceps.
- Flex your ankle of the bottom leg to prevent actively pushing off the floor, another compensation that reduces the effectiveness of the exercise.

- You can also increase the difficulty of this exercise by adding a load to one side of the body. This has the effect of adding a greater stability challenge to the exercise, emphasising the use of the core muscles to maintain form. Alternatively add a lunge movement in before the step for even greater challenge.

Petersen step up

Muscle focus – *vastus medialis oblique* (VMO)

Exercise 19	Petersen step up

This little-known exercise is aimed at strengthening the *vastus medialis oblique* (VMO). The VMO is the teardrop muscle on the inside of the thigh that you can see when you extend the leg and is often implicated in knee injuries due to its attachment onto the kneecap and role in decelerating knee flexion. Weakness in the quadriceps and poor movement at the knee joint (often related to the hip or ankle) are both a problem that this movement can help to solve. I was first shown this by Charles Poliquin and have found this exercise to be highly effective for anyone with knee problems or needing to improve knee joint stability.

- Begin with one foot up on a step with your heel raised and your foot turned out 15 degrees. To be effective, you **must** be on your toes with your heel raised as high as possible.
- Your lower leg is placed forward of the stance leg with the heel of it in line with the toes of the upper foot.
- Ensure that you keep your torso upright and raise the toes of your lower leg before beginning the movement.
- Step up onto the stance leg, extending through your knee joint and allowing your heel to move to the step.
- Pause in the balanced position before returning to the start of the movement.

It is easy to cheat on step ups and direct the movement elsewhere, this will be even more tempting if you are trying to strengthen a weak or injured knee. Common cheats include leaning forward from the hips or pushing off from the floor. If you are having to do this, reduce the load or step height. Continue with the exercise with added weight before increasing step height.

Supplemental exercises

Single leg calf raise

Muscle focus – *gastrocnemius*

Exercise 20	Single leg calf raise

Dedicated exercises for the calf muscles generally have one purpose and that is to build bigger calves! The calf muscles are genetically usually a good indicator of overall ability to build muscle, although with plenty of work they can be improved upon. They are usually trained using exercises such as the standing calf raise or the donkey calf raise, but can easily be trained using just a block of wood or step and a dumbbell. This exercise focuses on the *gastrocnemius*, the most superficial of the calf muscle group. The gastrocnemius is a predominantly fast-twitch muscle so, in order to get the best from the exercise, work with slightly shorter sets of 20–40 seconds.

- Start with a block or step positioned around 18–24 inches from a wall.
- Stand on the block with just the front part of your foot, allowing your heel to drop down fully.

- Ensure you maintain good alignment of the knee, hip, and spine to focus the effort on the calf. Use the wall to maintain balance as needed.
- Extend your ankle through a full range of motion, pause at the bottom of the movement and return to the start position.

Seated barbell calf raise

Muscle focus – *soleus*

Exercise 21	Seated barbell calf raise

The seated calf raise places the knee into a flexed position, which removes the *gastrocnemius* from the exercise and places greater emphasis on the *soleus*. The soleus is a deeper muscle that lies underneath the gastrocnemius and is also an ankle flexor. It is far more of a slow-twitch muscle and responds better to higher repetitions and longer sets. Aim to lift and lower for a count of at least four up and four down on each repetition to really hit this muscle hard.

You will again need a block of wood or small step for this exercise.

- Start seated on the end of a bench or chair with a barbell held across your knees.

- Your feet should be positioned with just the balls of your feet on the block or step and your ankle flexed.
- Slowly extend your ankle, pressing through the balls of your feet into a position of full extension.
- Return to the start position being sure to work through the complete range of movement.

Supine hip extension leg curl (SHELC)

Muscle focus – glutes, hamstrings

Exercise 22	SHELC

- From this position draw your heels in towards your backside and maintain the movement of hip extension as you do this, elevating your hips.
- Slowly control the movement back to the start position, lower the hips and then repeat.

The SHELC exercise is a simple movement for the hips, in particular the hamstrings, as well as also hitting the *gastrocnemius* in the calf. The leg curl movement works the hamstrings as a knee flexor in contrast to their role in the deadlifts where they work as hip extensors.

- Start in a supine position with your heels on a stability ball.
- Raise your hips off the floor, concentrating on squeezing the glutes to do this and taking care not to arch through your lower back.

Glute/ham raises

Muscle focus – hamstrings, glutes

Exercise 23	Glute/ham raises

Glute ham raises can be done on a specific machine, with a partner, or by improvising with a loaded barbell from which to anchor your feet. A big advantage of this exercise is the considerable overload it provides using only your bodyweight.

This exercise places a large eccentric demand on the hamstrings and can cause some pretty severe muscle soreness, so start off with 1–2 sets and work up from there.

- The start position is kneeling with your knees at a right angle and your feet anchored, either by a partner or by a well-weighted barbell. It is a good idea to pad the area beneath your knees to prevent stress to the kneecap.
- Slowly lower yourself towards the floor, controlling the descent by actively working the hamstrings. Maintain braced abdominals throughout this movement, keeping the glutes tight.
- Keep your arms to the front and as you cannot support yourself anymore, drop into the press-up position to protect your face from hitting the floor.
- Press explosively back up, working the hamstrings to get you back into the start position.

Summary

There are many ways you can tweak the previous exercises, simply select a version of the exercise most suited to what you wish to achieve.

Many of the lower body exercises shown can be combined with an upper body movement using dumbbells, medicine balls, or something similar in order to create a more total body challenge. While this will limit the amount of overload on the legs, it is an excellent way to increase the metabolic and motor skill demands of the exercise, adding interest and variety to the movement.

TOTAL BODY EXERCISES – AN INTRODUCTION TO THE OLYMPIC LIFTS

6

Total body training movements encapsulate free weights at their very best. These exercises simply cannot be performed on machines and they offer a far greater challenge to the metabolic, musculoskeletal, and neuromuscular systems than those exercises that target one specific plane, muscle, or pattern of movement. Unlike some of the more common exercises seen in health clubs, total body lifts have a large element of skill to them that needs to be achieved before using large loads. The importance of mastering technique in each exercise cannot be overstated, both for injury prevention and performance.

For this reason in particular, the full versions of the Olympic lifts have not been included in this book. In my experience it is virtually impossible to learn the correct execution of them without the help of a skilled coach to observe and correct technique. If you are really interested in progressing then it is well worth investing some time and money in sessions with a professional weightlifting coach.

While there is no doubting the many benefits of the full Olympic lifts, it is debatable how necessary they are for overall health and for some people the benefits will not outweigh the risks associated with them. There are many alternatives, such as initially learning the hang versions of the lifts, or performing them with dumbbells or kettlebells, which can add a unilateral challenge well suited to those with less than optimal mobility or without access to barbells and racks.

Warming up for total body movements

There are some simple additions to your warm up routine that you should consider performing before beginning your warm up sets. These movements can be performed using an unloaded barbell that will serve as good preparation for you before adding load to the bar.

Wrist extension/flexion mobility

The wrist joint can come in for a bit of a tough time with these exercises, particularly during the clean, which requires a good degree of wrist extension to perform correctly. Regular work on this area can soon bring about improvements.

The first thing to start with is some basic wrist mobility work before performing the clean position rack stretch.

- Begin with flexing and extending your wrists with your arms outstretched. Repeat this for 15–20 repetitions.
- Interlock your fingers and perform wrist rolls in a figure of eight pattern. Repeat for 15–20 repetitions.
- Move on to the clean position stretch.

Clean position rack stretch

The clean position rack stretch is an example of a stretch for a movement rather than simply for a muscle. Continued use of this will hit the area in the chain that is limiting mobility. This stretch also works well when performed as an active movement as well as a static stretch. You need a barbell for this racked at shoulder height.

- Assume the rack position as shown in the photo.
- Concentrate on driving your elbows upwards and forwards into an active stretch. You will feel this mainly through your forearms.
- Hold this position for 1–2 seconds.
- Ease out the stretch for 1–2 seconds and then back in.
- Repeat for a minimum of 8 repetitions as needed.

Cuban press in either snatch or clean position

This exercise combines the movement of an upright pull with a powerful rotation of the shoulders into the overhead position, strengthening the external rotators of the shoulder. Vary your performance of this movement between different grip widths. Start out with dumbbells before progressing to a barbell.

- Begin with the barbell held at your waist.
- Row it up to your sternum or till your upper arm is parallel with the floor.
- Rotate your shoulders bringing the bar overhead.
- Extend your arms to lockout.
- Lower under control and repeat.

Good mornings

The good morning teaches a principle that is **essential** for safe and effective lifting by focusing on the ability to rotate around the hip joints and **not** the lower back. Rounding the lower back whilst lifting a load is not recommended and prevents efficient force transfer of the powerful hip muscles.

- Take an unloaded barbell from the rack with it held in the same position as used in the back squat.
- Unlock your knees and keep your chest lifted through the movement.
- Bend forwards from your hips, maintaining an arch in the lower back and keeping your chest lifted throughout.
- Go as far forward as possible, letting your hips move back.
- Return under control, concentrating on moving through your hips and not overextending the lumbar spine.

This drill is limited by hamstring flexibility and will help develop an active range of movement in these muscles. As this can be difficult to sense, it is best performed with a spotter to monitor form or at worst with a mirror for self-correction. For photos of this exercise, see page 73.

Arms up front squat

Exercise I	Arms up front squat

This movement develops the concept of an upright trunk position that is essential in front squatting and Olympic style squatting.
- Take the barbell from the rack with it balanced across your shoulder muscles.
- Keep your arms raised to the front, parallel to the floor.
- Perform a squat in this position.
- To avoid dropping the bar, you must keep both your chin and chest up, and your torso as upright as possible.
- Repeat for 6–8 repetitions.

Snatch squat/overhead squat

The snatch squat can be both a humbling and revealing exercise. This has become a valuable assessment tool amongst strength coaches everywhere as it requires excellent mobility from the ankle through to the thoracic spine.

If you have a great difficulty with this movement then it is a sure sign of the need to make mobility a key focus of your training plan. You can begin by simply using a wooden dowel or broomstick before moving on to the barbell. If you find this a struggle, begin with a single arm version.
- Take the dowel/bar overhead with a wide snatch style grip.
- Keep your arms at full extension through the movement.
- Holding the bar in this position, squat as far as possible.
- Extend back to the start position and repeat for 6–8 repetitions.

This movement usually becomes a lot easier with a heel raise as this benefits both ankle mobility and shifts the centre of gravity forwards slightly, favouring a more upright position. While not a permanent solution, this can be of use for those who find this movement particularly challenging.

If preparing for a snatch workout, the wider grip can be used. Alternatively assume a standard width grip on the bar, similar to that used when performing a clean.

These warm up movements can be combined into a complex of movements along with a couple of the assistance exercises to make an ideal warm up routine. Try this selection before you begin your workout as a total body warm up with light weights. The exercises are performed for 3–5 reps, one after the other without any rest.
1. Deadlift from the hang or RDL x 3–5
2. Clean grip deadlift x 3–5
3. Muscle clean x 3–5
4. Upright pulls x 3–5
5. Cleans x 3–5
6. Front squat x 3–5
7. Overhead press x 3–5
8. Overhead squat x 3–5
Note: The muscle clean is a slower version

using only a bar or very light weights, where the bar is pulled up to the top of the chest (higher than in the normal explosive version) and the elbows then rotated through to the rack or overhead position, slower than in the normal version. You can perform a similar movement with a snatch grip, which trains mobility and rotation strength at the shoulder.

The hang clean

There is quite a bit of terminology to get used to with the Olympic lifts. Simply, any movement with the term hang used as a prefix indicates that the exercise begins with the bar held at the thigh, as opposed to the floor. This version of the full lifts requires far less technique and mobility and is easier to both teach and learn.

Before learning the hang clean it is a good idea to develop good overall strength, particularly in the posterior chain of the body (hamstrings, glutes, lower and upper back) that has such a big part to play in these lifts. Although technique plays a big part with these exercises, strength will become the limiting factor to performance if not developed. The best exercises to build strength for the clean are:

- Front squat
- High pulls
- Romanian deadlifts
- Deadlifts
- Good mornings

When you first begin to learn the clean and snatch it is best to use a lightly loaded barbell. I prefer this to a broomstick, as sometimes recommended, as a stick has so little inertia to overcome that it becomes hard to get a feel for the correct movement.

An adult man should be able to begin with an unloaded barbell, while a woman is best starting with a lighter bar, which usually weighs around 12–15kg.

Exercise 2   The hang clean

Learning the hang clean

Both the hang clean and hang snatch teach the essential principle of triple extension. This refers to a powerful explosion of the hips, knees, and ankles, similar to if you tried to jump as high as you could from a standstill.

For many, the trickiest part of the clean is mastering the rack position at the end of the lift, which requires good external rotation at the shoulder along with wrist extension to get the bar resting across the shoulders. A slight increase in grip width can help this, as can some work on wrist and shoulder mobility.

Another key point with the clean is that people often perform a version of this during group exercise classes, where it is often taught incorrectly. Both the clean and snatch are driven from the hips, not from the arms and this is essential to learn correctly if you are to gain the best results from the exercise. To keep it simple, I have broken the hang clean down into three parts, each of which links into the other to perform the lift smoothly and explosively.

The jump

- Start with your feet in the same position as for a deadlift and a grip just outside shoulder width. The overhand grip is suitable for most lifters, though some will progress to the hook grip later.
- Keep your arms locked straight, chest held high, and the bar close to your body.
- Keeping the bar on your thighs lower it to just above your knees, flexing at the knees and hips.
- Instantly reverse the movement, explode and actively try to jump upwards, extending through your ankles, knees, and hips. Shrug your shoulders forcefully, keeping the bar close to your body.

The pull

Now you have got the bar moving it is important not to let your arms bend too early, until you have fully extended through your hips as this will prevent transfer of force from the triple extension movement.

- By this point the bar will be around your belly button.
- Keeping the bar close to your body, your arms start to bend pulling you under the rising bar into the rack position.
- The classic mistake here is to either reverse curl or upright row the bar into the rack position. This is a mistake, as the bar must stay close to your chest as you begin to drop under it.

The rack

- To complete the lift requires a rapid drive forwards of your elbows, bringing the bar to rest on your shoulders.
- As you drive your elbows forwards and upwards, drop into a squat position to catch the bar across your shoulders in the same position as used for a front squat. This part of the movement takes a bit of practice to coordinate and must be done rapidly.
- Once the bar is strongly racked, extend from the ¼ squat back to complete the lift.
- Take care lowering the bar, reversing the movement and catching it back in the start position.

The hang snatch

The snatch is a tough exercise and one that demands mobility and stability particularly around the shoulder joint to be performed safely. You should be able to perform an overhead squat keeping the arms directly overhead and with the torso upright before performing this exercise with a load. Without the mobility needed to do this, the risk of shoulder injury is greatly increased and therefore efforts should be focused on developing the necessary range of movement before loading. However, the hang snatch is a great movement for developing real speed and explosive power, not to mention a really fun exercise.

Assistance exercises for the snatch movement are as follows:

- Overhead barbell squat
- Behind neck press
- Wide grip upright pulls
- Snatch grip Romanian deadlift
- Snatch grip deadlift

The big difference with the snatch is the wide grip placement used. This means that there is less distance for the bar to move overhead. This position demands excellent mobility at the

| Exercise 3a | The hang snatch |

| Exercise 3b | Kettlebell variation |

shoulder and some may prefer a slightly narrower grip if the weight is not near maximal. To find a snatch grip, bend over trapping the bar in the crease of the groin and stomach. Slide your hands along the bar until your elbows lock out and that is your snatch grip.

Learning the hang snatch

The jump

- Take the bar from the rack to the RDL position with a wide snatch grip.
- Keep your arms locked straight, chest held high, and the bar close to your body.
- Keeping the bar on your thighs lower it to just above your knees, flexing at the knees and hips.
- Instantly reverse the movement, explode and actively try to jump upwards, extending through your ankles, knees, and hips. Shrug your shoulders forcefully, keeping the bar close to your body.

The pull and catch

- Once you have extended through your hips, allow your arms to bend pulling yourself under the bar into a ¼ squat position.
- Keep pulling yourself under the bar and as it passes your head, drive your elbows forwards flipping the bar overhead.
- Extend your wrists backwards and take your arms straight to lockout – this is **not** a pressing movement.
- Extend from the squat position to fully upright, lowering the weight under control.

Mastering the last part of this lift can take some practice, particularly given its dynamic nature. Remember that the bar is taken overhead to a locked-out position in one rapid and explosive movement; it is not lifted to the shoulders and then pressed overhead. Like the clean, the temptation is to try to lift the bar with the arms rather than drive it with power from the legs and hips. The arms' role is to pull the body underneath the bar and then support it in the overhead position. Done correctly, the snatch is possibly the best free weight exercise that there is for developing total body explosive power.

The jerk

At first glance, the jerk may seem similar to the push press shown in the upper body chapter. However, it is far more explosive and more total body in nature. The main difference is that when performing a jerk movement the body is actually lowered underneath the bar, relying on the generation of explosive movement from the legs and hips to get the bar moving.

The most common version of this movement in competitive weight lifting is using the split jerk though you can also use a squat jerk where the feet remain in a square squat stance. Compared to its two more complex relatives, the jerk is a fairly basic movement that can be learnt quickly if you already have experience lifting overhead and have a solid military press on which to build. Basic assistance exercises for the jerk are as follow:

- Military press
- Push press
- Jump squats
- Overhead squat

Exercise 4a	The jerk

Learning the jerk

The jerk is a fairly straightforward lift, but with a few key points to remember that are shown below. Start with a relatively light weight or empty barbell at first to get a feel for the explosive aspect of this lift. The lift can be performed either with a split stance or a squat stance.

- Take the bar from the rack with a clean width grip or slightly wider with the bar as close to the heel of your hand as possible.
- Elbows are forwards and slightly downwards keeping your chest lifted.
- Keeping your torso upright dip into a ¼ squat position (don't go too far, this is a short explosive movement).
- Without hesitation explode upwards, driving the bar upwards and pushing your body underneath it.
- Lock the elbows out overhead.
- Extend your hips to an upright position.

Adding the split

Exercise 4b	The split

- As you drive the bar upwards explosively, split your feet with whichever foot feels most comfortable forwards.
- Lock your elbows out overhead.
- Push back to a squat stance from the front foot.

Kettlebell specific total body movements

Total body movements are not strictly limited to the Olympic lifts performed with a barbell. As we have already seen these lifts can be performed with dumbbells, or alternatively hybrid lifts can be developed combining two or three movements together as shown in Chapter 10. The impact of kettlebells on the modern fitness industry continues to grow as this book is being written and some of the movements used with KBs warrant inclusion here. If you haven't got a kettlebell to hand you can just as effectively use a dumbbell.

The swing

Exercise 5	The swing

This movement is probably the exercise most synonymous with the kettlebell and offers another way to develop hip extension and strengthen the body's posterior chain. Take care to hold a strong arch in the lower back and to keep the chest lifted throughout this movement.
- Begin with the bell held at arms' length with your legs wider than shoulder width apart,

glutes tight and abdominals braced.
- Keeping your back tight and the chest up, take the bell back between your legs.
- Thrust your hips forwards, whipping the bell upwards to a position with your arms parallel to the floor. Keep your glutes and abdominals tight through this movement.
- Allow the bell to drop back down between your legs keeping your back arched and abdominals tight.

The windmill

Exercise 6	The windmill

The windmill is all about shoulder stability and conditioning for the core of the body incorporating bending, twisting, and extending together in one multi-plane movement.
- Press the bell overhead keeping your arm contracted tight into the socket. Both your feet are then turned away from the arm the bell is in, at approximately 45 degrees, this is the start and finish position.
- The first movement is to push your hip (on the side of the bell) out to the side. This will cause the knee nearest to the bell to bend slightly. Your arm is straight and locked at

the elbow, as well as tight in the shoulder socket; your eyes are focused on the bell.

- Your body lowers and rotates, the arm not holding the bell (if not behind the back) crosses your body and moves towards the opposite foot, your eyes should remain on the bell.
- Push into the floor and extend your hips to lift and rotate them back in to the starting position, looking at the bell the whole time. Keep your arm straight and your shoulder tight and strong in the socket.

Turkish get up

This is a seriously challenging exercise that can take a bit of practice to get right. The TGU is another movement that really targets shoulder stability by challenging you to maintain a strong position with the kettlebell throughout a whole body movement.

- Start on your back with the kettlebell pressed directly overhead and your arm locked out straight.
- Bend the leg on the same side as the kettle-bell keeping your foot flat on the floor. Cross the other leg underneath and reach out to the side with your other arm.
- Drive the foot of the bent leg into the floor while pushing with the arm on the floor, keeping focused on the kettlebell at all times.
- Move onto one knee and then into a standing position. Reverse the movement to return to the start position.

As well as these challenging total body movements, kettlebells can also be used for exercises such as front squats, snatches, and cleans to provide a different challenge to both grip and stability. For the swing, men can begin with a 12kg bell and women an 8kg. For the windmill and get-up a slightly lighter bell is advised to begin with. Remember, if you don't have a kettlebell, you can always perform these with a dumbbell instead.

Exercise 7	Turkish get up

A word on abdominals or core training

There has been much discussion of core training and a review of it is beyond the scope of this book. The concept of stability and core training is relatively new and has gained much attention over recent years. However, what is certain is that strong abdominals and back muscles are important for successful weight training and can be developed in no small part through learning to squat, deadlift, press, and pull correctly with good form. The amount of isolated abdominal work required depends on the individual, although most people like to include it in some form into their training.

Those with a history of back problems or who are new to weight training will benefit from a progressive approach of dedicated abdominal and stability-oriented work before they progress on to more dynamic movements. However, it is important to understand that much like the rest of the body, the abdominals do not operate in isolation and as a result will also gain in strength and function through the use of whole body free weight exercises. Further reading on this topic is recommended in the bibliography.

One of the most effective methods of strengthening the mid-section is to perform exercises where one side of the body is loaded to a greater degree than the other. This generates a torque that must be effectively controlled by the trunk stabilisers for the exercise to be performed.

Make sure that when performing these movements you choose a load that is appropriate and not so high that successful completion of the movement is impossible. Unilateral exercises are best performed with sets of greater than 6 repetitions – generally between 12–20 are ideal during a stability phase of training.

Examples of challenging unilateral exercises are:
- Single arm chest press
- Single arm unsupported row
- Offset press-ups
- Unilaterally loaded step ups
- Walking lunge with weight held overhead
- Lunge and single arm overhead press

There are many different abdominal strengthening exercises that can target various aspects of the abdominal musculature. A selection of dedicated strengthening movements for the abdominals that cover the movements of the trunk – such as flexion/extension, lateral flexion, and rotation – are shown below.

Learning to brace the abdominals

The abdominal brace is a good place to start with abdominal exercises. It has the effect of creating a protective cylinder around the body that prevents the spine from buckling from its neutral position during lifting or movement. It also helps stiffen the body for effective force transfer, where it might activate rapidly to a high level for a brief duration during an explosive movement, such as a clean or snatch exercise. This feeling of bracing is similar to what you might do if bracing against a blow to the stomach.
- Find a neutral standing position where the lumbar muscles feel relaxed.
- Brace your abdominals gently as if about to stiffen against a jab to the stomach. This is not a maximal effort and should involve **no** spinal movement.
- Maintain good posture, ensuring that your chest is lifted and your chin is not poking forwards.
- Your abdominals should not be hollowed or swelled out.
- You should be able to feel an increase in the activity of the lumbar erectors as you do this.

Stability ball curl-up

Exercise 8	Stability ball curl-up

- Begin supine on the stability ball with a dumbbell held at the chin.
- With high levels of weight your feet may need to be anchored using a pair of heavy dumbbells.
- Lower back over the ball, extending your upper back and neck.
- Curl up to a position just above the horizontal beginning with the cervical spine and working down your back. This ensures strengthening of the cervical spine flexors as well as trunk flexors.
- Lower back under control and repeat for 2–3 sets of 6–10 reps.

The great thing about using the stability ball for a curl-up movement is that it allows the abdominals to be exercised through a full range of flexion to extension. This focuses more effort on the *rectus abdominis* and *obliques* instead of the hip flexors so often overworked in the conventional sit-up movement.

Adding weight allows for further strengthening of the abdominals through a lower rep range than is normally performed for the abs. I like to perform this with weight for between 6–10 repetitions, emphasising a controlled lowering with each rep.

Back extensions

Exercise 8	Back extensions

Where you position the pivot during this movement will dictate where the work is focused, a higher position works on the upper back, whereas a position under the hips works the whole posterior chain. If using a ball you may need to brace the feet under a barbell or bench. This movement can be performed using a stability ball, bench, or back extension bench depending on what is available.

- Position yourself so that movement occurs around the desired area.
- Lower yourself forwards keeping a neutral spine position.

- Rise back to the start position, taking care not to overextend your back.
- Perform sets of up to 20 reps as needed.

Rollouts

Exercise 9	Rollouts

Rollouts are great movements for challenging the isometric strength of the abdominals and building true core stability. This exercise targets the *rectus abdominis* and external *obliques* in particular and is an excellent way to develop a strong abdominal brace.

- Begin in a plank position with your hands on an Olympic bar, ensuring you have circular discs on the end.

- Keeping a strong abdominal brace, flex through your shoulders to roll the bar away from you.
- Maintain alignment through your hips and lower back.
- Roll the bar back in (using your abdominals, not your arms) and repeat for 8–12 reps.
- Once you can do it in this position, move into the full press-up position with your hands on the bar and repeat. (This is a **highly** advanced exercise.)

Russian twists

The Russian twist is an effective exercise for developing rotational stability and strength in the abdominals.

- Lie supine on the floor using two heavy dumbbells as anchors for your arms.
- Raise your legs, keeping a slight bend at the knee. Ensure you keep your shoulder blades in contact with the floor at all times.
- Lower your legs to one side, bracing your abdominals to control this movement.
- Work through the mid-section to bring your legs back up to vertical, lower to the opposite side.
- Repeat for 8–12 reps each side.

Exercise 10	**Russian twists**

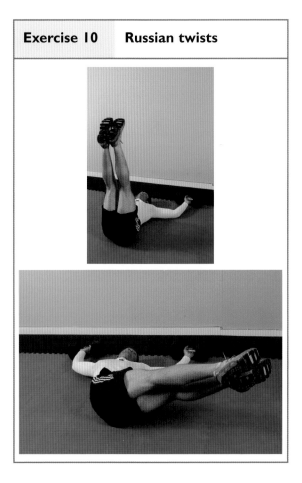

Side bridge

Exercise 11	**Side bridge**

The side bridge trains the *obliques* and *quadratus* while sparing the load on the back in a far better way than something like a seated abdominal twist, or loaded side bend. It can be used either with isometric holds of 30s–2 minutes or for repetitions as desired.

• Lie on one side with your legs together and elbow on the floor directly under your shoulder.
• Keep your abdominals activated and your hips slightly pressed forwards into extension.
• Elevate your mid-section off the floor.
• Hold for 1 minute and repeat on the opposite side.

Summary

This chapter is an introduction to the total body Olympic movements using the easiest variations. However, these can still be very effective at developing your strength-speed. The movements can be adapted for all and can just as easily be performed using dumbbells or kettlebells. This is a technically less demanding option that is also suited to higher repetition work, as part of a circuit or metabolic training phase. The full barbell versions should never be performed for more than six repetitions, as the postural fatigue this causes is likely to be detrimental to technical performance.

PART **THREE**

Plan your work, then work your plan

Getting results is what weight-training is all about, whatever your training goals. Without results, training starts to stagnate, motivation drops, and it can all start to become hard work. Successful strength coaches are judged firstly on their results, then their resume.

An understanding of how to manipulate the basic variables is a pre-requisite for success when training with free weights. Randomly applying a wide range of methods is unlikely to result in any great gains, not to mention making it near impossible to track progress. Whether you train on purely Olympic lifts, kettlebells or for bodybuilding, this principle remains the same. The subject of programme design has, and continues to be, the sole subject of many texts and courses and a complete discussion on the topic is well beyond the scope of this book. However, while there is considerable research and science on the matter, an understanding of some simple and well-established principles is all that is needed for you to design your own effective training programme.

There are essentially three main types of resistance training, which can then be further sub-divided into various different training approaches.

Three methods are shown below.
- Maximal efforts – the use of maximal or near maximal weights.
- Repeated efforts – lifting a sub-maximal weight for repeated efforts until reaching muscular failure.
- Dynamic efforts – lifting a sub-maximal weight with the greatest possible amount of speed.

Depending on your training goals, training age, and other variables these methods may form the basis of either a single workout or an entire phase of training. Similarly, they may be trained together in a training phase or even in a single workout. Ideas on how to do this effectively will be presented in this section along with some suggested training programmes, to allow you to design and develop your own training programmes based around an understanding of some simple principles.

Of course each coach has their own philosophy on weight training, in the same way that each person has their own goals, or each sport has unique conditioning needs. Training for these means comes from the research, but more often from the experiences of the coach in what has and hasn't worked for them in the past.

These different approaches share some common truths and these are always best reflected in the bare basics of the training programme that deals with the major acute exercise variables that are:
- Repetitions
- Sets
- Rest intervals
- Tempo of movement
- Exercise selection

- Training frequency and split
- Periodisation of training and recovery

So, let's start with what is regarded as the most fundamental of the acute training variables.

Repetition, repetition, repetition . . .

When it comes to designing a training programme, many people will sit down and try to come up with exercises first. This is usually a mistake.

The first and most important exercise variable to consider is the amount of repetitions to be performed per set of exercise.

There are a few reasons why this is the case. Firstly, the amount of repetitions that we perform will dictate the training *intensity* and therefore the adaptation in the various systems of the body. In turn this will dictate the various other parameters such as rest periods, tempo of movement, number of sets, and exercise choice.

Secondly, the number of repetitions is the variable to which we adapt the fastest in any workout. Leading strength coaches generally agree that the body adapts to any given workout in as little as **six** exposures to it.

The repetition continuum

The effect of any given number of repetitions can be shown as part of what is called the repetition continuum and are typically talked about in relation to what is called the repetition maximum or RM.

1RM = The maximum amount of weight that you can lift in one attempt.
12RM = The maximum amount of weight you can lift for 12 repetitions in one single set.

It should be fairly obvious that lifting a weight that is your 1RM will have a significantly different training effect to lifting a weight you can perform for 12 repetitions. This means that the number of repetitions you select will greatly affect the outcome of your training and should be matched to your training goals for the best outcome. For example, developing relative strength is best done with sets of 1–5 repetitions using a weight that will be between 85–100% of your 1RM. Conversely, if you wish to target the local endurance of a movement pattern or muscle group then sets of 15 or more repetitions would be more appropriate.

Figure 7.1 overleaf shows the wide range of effects possible by altering the repetition bracket, with each effect either growing or diminishing depending upon which direction you move along the continuum. For example, sets of 6–8 repetitions target a more functional type of muscle hypertrophy with a greater emphasis on high force production and fast-twitch fibre recruitment. In contrast, sets of 12–16 tend to develop greater muscle endurance by targeting the slower-twitch motor fibres and generating higher levels of lactate in the muscles.

A repetition need not just be straight up and down. Using a technique known as a 1 ¼ rep can help to increase the time spent in the hardest part of the lift, developing more tension in the muscle at that point, increasing the growth stimulus, and generating higher levels of lactate. A set of squats like this and your quads will be on fire!

To perform a 1 ¼ rep, simply lower the weight down to the bottom of the movement, come up a ¼ of the way, go back down to the bottom and then come all the way up. Simple, but very effective.

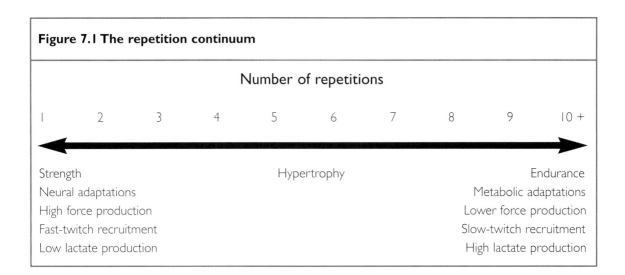

Figure 7.1 The repetition continuum

Factors affecting the repetition continuum

Several factors can affect the amount of repetitions that can be performed at any given time, such as the following:

- The function of the muscle. Predominantly slow-twitch muscles such as the soleus or the quadriceps can hypertrophy on as many as 50 repetitions, conversely the hamstrings respond better to low (6–8) reps for hypertrophy, as they are more fast-twitch in nature.
- Training age. Those new to training will improve their strength on as many as 16–20 repetitions as they learn how to lift, while a more experienced athlete will respond to a smaller range of reps to increase strength. In general, a minimum of 70% of your 1RM will be necessary for improvements in strength. Any less than this will not provide a strong enough stimulus for change.
- Genetic make-up. People with a bias to fast-twitch motor units will respond far better to low repetition ranges than those with a more slow-twitch makeup, they will also have variations in recovery rate and hormonal make-up as well.

It is for these reasons and several others that using the number of repetitions as a guide to desired adaptations is more useful than a given percentage of your maximum (%RM). Training alters many different factors, such as exercise order, frequency, repetition speed, rest intervals, circadian variations, and even the type of exercise. This means your actual 1RM can change on a daily basis. Also, percentages of 1RM are not constant for each different lift, so you may be able to perform significantly different numbers of repetitions according to which exercise is selected. The repetition continuum provides a solid guide by which to select your best training range for the desired results and should then be combined with the following variables to complete your training programme.

Sets

Now you have decided upon how many repetitions you need to perform per set for your desired results, it is time to decide how many sets to perform per workout. Again, there is a simple rule of thumb for this, which you should follow (with a few exceptions).

The number of sets you perform will be inversely related to the number of repetitions.

Standard practice in the weights room for many years was to perform three sets for any given exercise. The advice of the American College of Sports Medicine is that for general health and well-being you should perform 1–2 sets of 8–10 exercises, a prescription that while it is well meaning is not likely to be suitable for continued improvement or gains in strength and muscle after the initial period of training. The exception to this has been found in older adults (65 years +) who have been found to make comparable improvements in muscle function and other measures of functional health when using single-set routines. However, a study on well-trained post-menopausal women found that over a longer period (8 months) those who used single-set routines actually decreased in strength. There is clear evidence that, for the largest share of the population, in particular those who are looking to develop muscular hypertrophy, strength, or power, multiple sets per exercise is necessary for improvements.

When you are training to develop neural adaptations in the body – such as when trying to improve your maximal strength – a low number of repetitions are used with a higher number of sets in order to gain sufficient exposure to the stimulus. Anything up to 10 or 12 sets per exercise for relative strength is common (some such as Bulgarian wave loading use up to 20 or 30 sets). When training for hypertrophy and using a higher rep range, slightly fewer sets will be employed due to the greater volume of repetitions used with each set (typically around 3–8 sets per exercise). Although some texts and magazines talk about single-set training, research studies have consistently shown that when training for strength, power, hypertrophy, or high-intensity endurance, multiple set approaches are more effective.

As with repetition prescription it is important to remember that when it comes to deciding how many sets you perform, you should tailor the workout to your own needs. An example of this is that the number of sets will dictate the total volume of the workout (sets x reps = total reps performed) and that this will have an impact on the trainee. It is important that to prevent overtraining you cut back on the sets at regular intervals. This will be even more necessary for those who train more often or at higher levels and are therefore far more prone to develop the signs of overtraining. To avoid this follow the simple rule below.

For advanced trainees or those who train regularly (more than 3 times a week), every 4th week cut your sets back by 30–40% for a week.

For intermediate trainees or those who train less regularly (up to 3 times a week) every 6th week cut your sets back by 30–40% for a week.

As with everything else, these rules are not set in stone, they are simply guidelines. It is important that you **never** sacrifice the quality of your training to achieve greater volumes of work, as this will never be beneficial. More is not always better.

Remember, the number of sets shown in a programme refer to the *work sets* as opposed to lighter warm-up sets that are not done to fatigue or failure. These should be performed to raise levels of neural activation, mental focus, and muscle metabolism ready for the work sets and should NOT interfere with performance.

Rest intervals

Though you may not think of it at first, choosing the right rest period for your training programme can have a dramatic effect on the outcome. Yet, along with tempo, this has to be the most overlooked aspect of many training programmes.

The simple reason for this is that the amount of rest you take between sets will determine whether or not you are able to recover from the previous set. Different length sets will tend to target a specific type of energy system. As well as fatiguing our energy systems we can also fatigue the nervous system when performing repetitions in the neural adaptation range. The nervous system can take up to six times longer to recover than the metabolic system and this should be given due consideration when the goal is to train maximum strength.

In general though, the rest period allows our other energy systems to get to work on replenishing the energy that was used to perform the set. This is also what happens after a particularly hard workout when energy sources within the body have been severely depleted and it is often referred to as repaying the oxygen debt. A simple example of this is to imagine sprinting up two or three flights of stairs. Although this might only take 10 or 20 seconds it can leave us breathing heavily afterwards. This is the body sucking in oxygen to replenish the rapid

demand for energy that was required for the burst of activity. Recently many fitness experts have given considerable importance to the use of the oxygen debt (called excess post-exercise oxygen consumption or EPOC) for fat loss although opinions about this are still divided. However, given that our resting metabolism accounts for around 75% of our total calorie expenditure it would seem logical that if we can raise the level at which it is working for a sustained period, then that could positively affect weight loss efforts. Studies have shown that high-intensity resistance training can lead to an EPOC effect lasting for well beyond 24 hours!

For some simple guidance on how long your rest period should be, let's refer to the repetition continuum below.

When rest periods are considered in relation to the other exercise variables they basically select themselves. For example, using the above figure we can see that if our goal is to work on strength then we would be using predominantly neurally adapting fast-twitch fibres, which fatigue easily. We also know that we would be

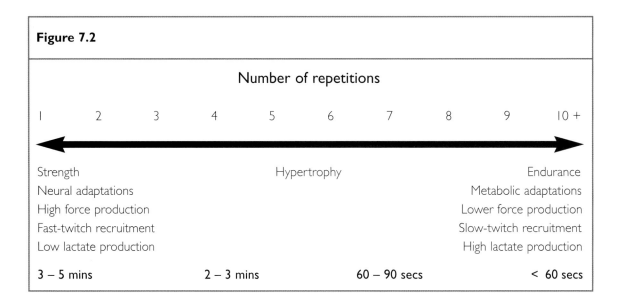

Figure 7.2

Number of repetitions

| 1 | 2 | 3 | 4 | 5 | 6 | 7 | 8 | 9 | 10 + |

Strength   Hypertrophy   Endurance

Neural adaptations   Metabolic adaptations

High force production   Lower force production

Fast-twitch recruitment   Slow-twitch recruitment

Low lactate production   High lactate production

3 – 5 mins   2 – 3 mins   60 – 90 secs   < 60 secs

targeting the short-term energy system, which requires at least three minutes to recover. We can also see that the aim is to achieve changes in the neural system of the body rather than to stress the metabolic system. For that reason longer rest periods of 3–5 minutes would be indicated.

However, when training for hypertrophy things are a bit different. We would use a lower load, therefore shorter rest periods would be indicated to sufficiently recruit and fatigue muscle fibres enough for a growth stimulus to occur. For that reason a rest period of around 60–90 seconds would be indicated between sets.

Remember, exercises with a high demand on the body in terms of complexity or coordination that are aimed at developing the nervous system (maximal and relative strength, explosive power, plyometrics, skills) cannot be performed optimally under fatigue and are reliant on a high contribution from the fast-twitch muscle fibres. For that reason, sufficient rest is required between sets. This may be a difficult concept for some, particularly those aerobically trained or from a group exercise background where the emphasis tends to be on getting a good sweat on. In general, rest intervals are largely down to common sense, though certain more obvious factors play a part. For example, the bigger the lifter the longer the rest period needed. Also, exercises that work large muscle groups (such as deadlifts and squats) or that require complex movement (such as cleans and snatches) will need longer rest intervals than small muscle group movements (such as abdominals or bicep curls).

Rest intervals can also be taken between repetitions in a set, although this is a far less practised technique. Resting for a short time between each repetition can allow partial recovery of the highest-threshold motor fibres allowing a greater volume of training to be performed at a higher intensity than would be possible if performing the repetitions continuously. This is the theory behind a technique called cluster and rest-pause training, described in Chapter 8.

Tempo or speed of movement

Along with rest intervals, tempo has to be the most frequently abused exercise variable that there is. Yet, the impact of moving a weight slowly or quickly, or changing the speed at which you lower a weight can have a significant influence on the training effect of the set and workout.

Although using different speeds has been around for quite a long time (the old saying, go slow to grow, is an example of this), the formalisation of this technique was popularised by Australian strength expert Ian King and Canadian Charles Poliquin. Although some coaches prefer a more pragmatic approach to timing, preferring instead to work to simple instructions such as slow, very slow, explosive etc, it would be hard to argue against the importance of some kind of tempo prescription if you are to make a movement specific to a desired training effect.

This is reinforced by considering the relationship between force and velocity. The force/velocity curve tells us that high velocities of movement do not elicit high levels of force. This can be a bit tricky to understand at first, but a simple example would be to consider the difference in trying to throw a tennis ball compared to a cannonball. While the tennis ball is light and relatively easy to throw at high speed, you would not need to apply high levels of force to do this. In contrast, the cannonball would need high levels of force simply to move even at a very slow velocity.

So what speed should you train at? Well, this is a complex subject but if we consider the principle of specificity then it would make sense to train at the speed at which the movement is going to be performed in the sports or everyday activity. So, this would suggest that to improve your vertical jump score (a commonly applied athletic test of power), you should only employ explosive jump training with little or no added weight. However, if your vertical jump ability is limited not by your *explosive* strength but by your actual ability to activate your fast-twitch fibres, then it is clear that unloaded jump training will not make a significant improvement to performance. In this case maximal strength improvements would be advised using greater loads and slower movements to activate the higher threshold motor fibres. In contrast, if an athlete is very strong but under-performs on explosive tests of power, then training for explosive strength would be indicated. This is known as improving the explosive strength deficit. In general, a stronger person will have a higher potential for explosive strength. Although as can be seen in racquet sports, only so much strength is necessary for the ability to hit the ball hard, hence overall strength will be less important than speed and skill. This is another example of the importance of understanding specificity in sport and training.

Controlling tempo also has many other benefits. Beginners for example, tend to rush their sets and controlling tempo forces them to recruit stabilising muscles and learn to perform their movements with perfect technique. It can also help by preventing the use of momentum during an exercise. Momentum is, of course, a functional strategy in most sports movements, but is not ideal for many aspects of strength training as it allows lifters to cheat on exercises and prevents the development of strength at the weakest part of the movement. Momentum can also reduce the need for high levels of muscle tension, such as those necessary to activate the highest threshold muscle fibres. It does this by activating what is known as the stretch reflex in

the muscle and using stored elastic energy to perform the concentric phase of the movement.

There are other important aspects to controlling tempo, as not all movements in life or sport are about lifting a weight (or concentric work). Many muscles and movements require excellent ability to either decelerate or absorb a weight (eccentric strength), or hold/resist movement in a given position (isometric strength). Controlling tempo allows due emphasis to be given to phases of the movement other than simply the concentric phase. This is of importance to anyone keen to improve strength or muscle size, as large gains in both can come from emphasising the eccentric phase of the movement.

An important differential does need to be made here between moving a weight slowly because it is very heavy, or moving a weight intentionally slowly to give due emphasis to a certain phase.

Lifting a heavy weight slowly can actually increase explosive strength. Despite what we said about specificity of movement, the reason for this is that many adaptations to this are neural. Therefore, if our *intention* is to move the weight as fast as possible, the adaptation will reflect that. This technique is also applied in bodybuilding, where lifters are instructed to focus on squeezing the muscle through the entire contraction in an effort to develop higher levels of activation in the muscle.

Of course, some exercises can *only* be performed at a certain speed. For example the hang clean can only be performed explosively as its success relies on generating enough speed to complete the *racking* of the bar. This is true for all the Olympic lifts, which are explosive by their very nature.

So we can see that tempo of movement is much like the other variables in that it is specific to the outcome you want from the exercise. It is also the same in that it needs to be varied to maintain adaptations and to prevent a plateau in training. It should be remembered though that intentionally moving a light weight slowly has little place outside the specific bodybuilding or certain rehabilitation techniques where reducing joint loading and forces is a prime consideration.

The system used in this book to describe lifting tempo is a four-number code such as the following:

3 1 2 1

- In this system the first number refers to the lowering or eccentric phase of the movement. In this case it would mean lowering the bar or weight for a count of 3 seconds, eg, lowering to the floor in a press-up.
- The next number refers to the pause taken in the stretched or bottom position of the movement, eg, holding in the bottom position of the press-up.
- The third number refers to the length of the concentric or shortening phase of the exercise, eg, pressing back up during the press-up exercise. This number may sometimes be replaced with the letter X to indicate that you perform the movement as fast as possible.
- The last number refers to the pause taken after the contracted phase. In the press-up this would be with the arms locked out at the top of the movement.

We would then pause for a count of two in the easiest position (in this exercise it is easiest to pause between eccentric and concentric phases) to allow the fast-twitch fibres to recover. Then we press the weight overhead as explosively as possible, before lowering again for a count of 4.

Of course, as is always the case, not everyone agrees with the use of such a strict system. They may have a point in some cases, for example research shows that people tend to score highest in tests on exercises such as push-ups and chin-ups when they select their own tempo. Some coaches prefer a more informal method,

opting for simply using slow lowering or explosive movement and you might well prefer this. However, we should remember that tempo is a variable that we can change to get different training effects, therefore the more specific the variable, the more specific the adaptation. It is up to you to find what system works best for you in this respect.

Volume, intensity, and density – understanding some often misused terms

Before we get into the importance of volume, first it is important to clarify a couple of terms often used in the weight-training world, usually incorrectly. As we will see, these terms have a fair bit of significance when understanding and discussing volume.

Intensity is often confused with density, yet the two are generally opposing in what they mean. When a workout is referred to as being high-intensity this should be taken to mean that it is performed using weights close to the 1RM. These types of workout usually focus on developing some form of maximal strength. Conversely a workout high in density is when the volume of work performed in that session is high, although not of a particularly high intensity. For example, a typical bodybuilders programme (typically consisting of a high number of sets at around 70–80% RM) could be referred to as high-density but **not** high-intensity.

We have already touched on volume when discussing sets, and it is an important variable to consider as excessive amounts of volume can prevent you from ever actually showing their true potential. Fatigue is a side-effect of lifting weights and contributes to reduced levels of performance. Constant use of high-volume routines without some sort of respite is a sure way to progressively fatigue and be in a constant state of overtraining. This is one of the prime reasons for periodisation.

Setting exact parameters for what constitutes exact levels of total volume is difficult as what may be too high for one person may be optimal for another. For example, someone well trained will typically need higher volumes of exposure to a stimulus compared to a beginner in order to see results, whereas someone who is a novice can progress happily within their tolerance levels without needing to work at the kind of levels that would be excessive. Similarly someone who is a predominantly fast-twitch trainee will need far lower volumes compared to a slow-twitch type individual, which also calls for different types of approach to programming. This may explain why this topic is somewhat glossed over in all but the most purist of strength training books and manuals.

When considering total volume, factors such as muscle groups, fibre types, intensity, nutrition and supplementation, frequency, phase of training, level of athlete, and use of anabolic substances can all make a difference. Workouts may vary from between 10 sets up to as many as 40, and it can be easy to get locked into doing 3 x 10 on everything. This means that the goalposts for volume can be a fair distance apart. So, when designing your programme here are a few pointers.

Novices – generally perform between 12 and 20 sets per workout.

Intermediates – generally perform between 15 and 25 sets per workout.

Advanced Lifters or those in specialisation phases – generally perform between 20 – 30 sets per workout.

Doing too much is a common problem, particularly for the lifter who always equates more as being better. After an hour in the gym your hormonal system will be sliding away from an anabolic state as your testosterone levels drop. Keeping workouts to below 60 minutes is not only better for growth stimulus, but also for exercise adherence and practicality!

As complex as it might all seem, if you play by the rules mentioned for the previous acute variables and by using some planning then you should be able to avoid any problems. To help with your programme design methods here are some general guidelines for the overall volume of your programme.

- High volume and high-intensity together should generally be avoided, as should low volume and low-intensity combinations.
- Regular back off strategies should be employed to allow for recovery and adaptation. The higher the volume or intensity, the more frequent these are required. For example, during a strength phase every fourth week reduce training volume by up to 40%.
- As a rule, the lower the intensity used, the higher the total repetitions used per exercise. When working at high intensities, more sets are required to expose the nervous system to adequate stimulus.
- The more exercises – the fewer the sets per exercise.
- Without chemical help, few people can regularly tolerate over 30 sets per workout – not to mention the time limitations of this.
- Cut back on volume rather than intensity to prevent overtraining.
- Smaller exercises allow for a greater amounts of sets.
- Beginners can tolerate lower levels of volume than experienced lifters.
- Follow the principles outlined previously with sets, reps, and rest to help guide total volume.

Opinions tend to vary on optimal ratios for volume, as they are dependant on such a wide variety of factors. This is clearly a tricky balance to achieve as many research projects on the effects of certain set/rep routines have been confounded by not considering the implications of total training volume. Too much volume and you risk overtraining, while too little and you risk getting no training effect at all. This has been shown to be true in the research too, with researchers able to actually induce overtraining and compare it to the levels that showed performance increases.

Exercise frequency – how often to train?

For many recreational trainees, how often to train can be dictated by commitments to work, family, friends, and other social pursuits, rather than selection of the optimal routine. The average health club member may lift weights 2–3 times a week, while a professional athlete may train twice daily with free weights. Training frequency can have an important bearing on the outcome of any training programme and should always be considered as one of the acute variables in programme design.

Many bodybuilders are able to train daily, simply through targeting individual muscle groups with each workout, working them to total fatigue and then effectively resting them for 5–7 days before repeating that workout. However, whether this approach is well suited to athletes or recreational trainees who have little need for such focus on individual muscles and tend to focus on movements or total body workouts is questionable and the topic of much contention among strength coaches, not least because of the extreme levels of soreness, known as DOMS, that this can induce for several days after. Some strength coaches believe muscle group bases approaches to be both outdated and ineffective in the training of complex movements, while others still successfully use this format.

So, how often should you be training? Well, there are some fairly general rules that research has shown us that, along with a number of other factors, can help you select the right approach.

Studies have shown that optimal gains from strength training tend to differ, particularly between trained and untrained lifters. However, between 3–5 days a week seems optimal with the upper body tending to respond better to greater frequency (5 days a week). A more frequent training approach allows greater specificity of training and more specialised methods, while someone training only once or twice a week should not expect the same types of progress due to the more generic nature of their programme. Before you select your own training frequency consider the following points:

- Total life stress. Although working out often represents a positive stressor in your life, it is a stressor no less. People under large amounts of adrenal stress should be wary of the potential for adrenal exhaustion through high levels of training frequency.
- Other types of training. If free weights are a supplemental aspect of your training programme then you need to be aware of the effects that other training can also have on the body. For example, if you perform a large amount of aerobic training, this is likely to have negative effects on your strength development as well as raising the potential for overtraining.
- Diet and lifestyle. If you do not eat, sleep, and live your life like an athlete, then it makes little sense in trying to try to train like one. You cannot expect to perform while hung-over or having just finished a burger and chips before the workout. Tolerating greater frequency of training requires a more focused approach to recovery, meaning that your nutrition needs to be a prime concern.
- Supplementation. Following on from the previous point, supplementation can be invaluable in aiding recovery and obtaining the essential nutrients needed to support your training. There is little point training for hypertrophy if you only eat 1200

calories a day. Getting the 4000 or so you may need for muscle growth through an optimal diet may be difficult, but through the use of protein shakes or meal replacement drinks this becomes possible. Other supplements are popular for helping recovery (such as glutamine and magnesium), or for reducing inflammation (fish oil), improving work tolerance (creatine), controlling free-radicals (vitamin E), aiding muscle growth (branch-chain amino acids), controlling cortisol (phosphotidylserine) or promoting testosterone by reducing excess oestrogen or natural boosters (DIM, maca, tribulus).

- Type of training used. The actual training methodology can make a big difference to the frequency you use when training with it. An example of this is supra-maximal eccentric training, which is likely to cause high levels of muscle soreness and neural stress that will require longer recovery periods. Similarly, a general preparation phase of training in the pre-season is likely to have greater frequency of training than a maintenance programme carried out during the competitive season.
- Goals. What you want out of your training programme will place a large emphasis on the required frequency. If you are training merely to benefit general health then a whole-body approach 1–3 times a week will have some limited benefits. If you are looking to reach the next Mr Olympia however, it is far from sufficient. Match your training frequency to your desired training outcomes.
- Training age. As previously discussed, the more experienced an athlete becomes, training frequency will increase, although this is, of course, proportional to their sport and training approach. Some Bulgarian weight lifting programmes have even involved several training sessions a day, although this is a highly specific approach and not appropriate for everyone.
- Individual differences. The importance of individualising your training carries across into training frequency. Listen to your body and use common sense when designing your training programme to allow for adequate recovery. Remember, sometimes less is more and a reduction in training frequency is needed to manifest improvements.

A note on supplementation

Mention supplementation to many and it will immediately arouse thoughts of the dark world of anabolic steroids – synthetically produced versions of the sex hormones such as testosterone, popularised by bodybuilders for surpassing their genetic potential for muscle growth. However, for most athletes use of supplements other than steroids has become essential for a wide range of roles. They include vitamins and minerals, amino acids, plant extracts, and herbs and are used across all the bodily systems. They can help to balance hormonal levels, increase available energy substrates, protect against cell damage, and many other different aspects of the metabolism.

Despite those who are critical of supplements, it is difficult with food production methods and soil quality to gain everything you need through diet alone, particularly if you require a specific type of nutrient. While it has become a multi-million pound industry, it is now also recognised as an essential part of an athlete's routine to use supplements.

Selecting and ordering the exercises

Finally in this chapter we come to the practice of selecting and ordering the exercises. This is the last of the exercise variables that is considered, as this will almost always be the case when designing a training programme. There are several established practices in this area of programme design, some of which are discussed in the individual programming methods in the following chapter. However, some simple guidelines can help with selection of exercises and the order in which to perform them.

- Perform explosive and dynamic exercises early in the workout. These exercises tend to be highly demanding on all systems of the body and should always be performed while you are at your freshest. For example, you should perform power cleans (highly explosive and complex movement) before a bicep curl (very low demands for energy or coordination).

- Perform complex movements before simple. Similarly, complex movements become harder to perform under conditions of fatigue, often leading to poor technique and undesirable patterns of movement.

- Exercise weakest areas first. The temptation can be to load a programme with all your favourite (ie, strongest) movements first. This can often be seen in the average gym on a Monday night where most people are working chest and arms. This only makes your strong movements stronger and your weak movements weaker, creating imbalances and ultimately injury. Always perform your weakest movements early in the workout or training schedule.

- Balance movements unless you are deliberately creating imbalance. As a rule it is wise to keep workouts balanced. However, this is simply achieved by alternating upper body with lower body workouts, or alternating pushing with pulling movements. The exception is where you might deliberately perform greater amounts of one type of movement to correct an existing imbalance.

- Hit the big exercises first and little ones last. Again, this rule is not without exception in the case of pre-fatigue routines, but as a rule, you should always perform large muscle group movements (squats, deadlifts, presses) before smaller muscle group movements (curls, scaptions, leg curls, tricep dips).

- Pick the right exercise for the sets/reps selected. As shown in Part Two, certain movements are best suited for specific goals. Exercises such as power cleans and snatches should not be performed for high repetition/strength endurance sets as they are specifically aimed at improving explosive strength. When performed for high reps, the postural muscles needed to perform these movements correctly tire, leading to poor form. Similarly, when trying to build maximal strength levels, performing the exercise on an unstable surface is not wise. Use common sense to select the right type of movement for the sets/reps/tempo selected.

- Highest intensity to lowest. Remembering that intensity is a direct equivalent of the percentage of 1RM, this means that we perform those movements at high levels of intensity earlier in the workout then lower ones. An example of this would be a mixed-fibre type workout that might look like this.

5 x 5 / 3 x 10 / 2 x 20

Follow these basic rules and you should be able to comfortably select the right exercise for the chosen exercise variables.

Summary

Selecting your repetitions, sets, and rest intervals should be the first step to designing your training programme, as it is these variables that dictate how your body will adapt to the routine. Once these have been selected it is then easier to select the exercises to match.

In the next section we will look at ways of organising sets and reps (and some of the other variables) using a range of methods. Remember, when selecting your acute variables, simply decide upon the desired outcomes of the programme and then use the repetition continuum to select the appropriate rep range, sets, rest, tempo, and frequency. Then find the right exercises to match those variables and you are well on your way. Done this way, programme design can be a simple task that can greatly affect your results.

PROGRAMME DESIGN

Part 2 – Spice up your sets and reps

Methods for increasing size, strength, or power

All too often training programmes become regimented to performing 2–3 sets of one exercise before moving on to the next movement in the programme. Although this might be simple, it is not a very efficient, versatile, or particularly exciting method of training.

There will of course be times when a simple sequence of exercises such as this is warranted but there are many, many different ways to organise and arrange your training days to get more proverbial bang for your buck.

In this section, we will look at many different methods of arranging sets and reps for specific results. Some of these methods are fairly popular and well-used while others may be new to you. Far from being new, most of them have also been in existence for a long time. I would encourage you to incorporate them into your training where appropriate. Many of these methods have their origins in bodybuilding or weightlifting, so you should use what is appropriate for your training needs and remember that these are usually more intensive methods and not all of them should be used by novices to weight training. Avoid the temptation to include too many different methods in a programme. They will simply counteract the effect and lead to confusion.

Supersets

The use of supersets is so simple and effective that I am amazed everyone does not use them in some form while training. This is hardly a new invention either and has been around for many years. Not only can supersets add variety to your workouts, but they can also be a valuable tool for getting greater amounts of work done during the time spent at the gym.

Supersetting simply refers to performing two exercises together in sequence, usually for opposing movement patterns or muscle groups (performed together for the same movement or muscles is known as pre or post-fatiguing – shown later). Rest intervals between supersets will be dependant on the desired goal of the programme, although care must be taken to combine suitable exercises, as many multi-joint movements have overlapping patterns of muscle recruitment.

Supersets are ideal, even for the novice trainee, as a way of increasing the efficiency of your workout time, adding interest as well as reducing the time spent resting.

Table 8.1 is a typical superset combining a lower body and upper body movement. The letters A1 and then A2 indicate that one exercise should be performed after another.

Table 8.2 is a superset that combines a pushing movement with a pulling movement. Interestingly research has shown that combining agonist/ antagonist movements such as this can lead to improved performance.

Table 8.1

Sequence	Exercise	Reps	Sets	Tempo	Rest
A1	Front squats	10–12	3	3020	60 sec
A2	DB bench press	10–12	3	3020	60 sec

Table 8.2

Sequence	Exercise	Reps	Sets	Tempo	Rest
A1	Chins	4–6	4	40X0	90 sec
A2	Military press	4–6	4	40X0	90 sec

Be careful not to combine exercises with overlapping demands or that place great emphasis on the lower back and core muscles to provide adequate support as this may result in a compromised performance on exercise A2. Therefore combinations of these overlapping movements should not be performed, as below.

A1 Barbell deadlifts
A2 Barbell back squats

However, as with everything there are some exceptions. Giant sets combine three movements all of similar movement patterns to maximally fatigue a muscle. To prevent problems with overlap, exercises should be selected that don't all fatigue the stabilising muscles, such as those performed seated for example.

Tri-sets and giant-sets

A progression from using supersets is to combine more than two movements into what is known as a tri-set or a giant set. Usually a tri-set would combine different movement patterns or muscle groups, while a giant set might figure three different exercises all aimed at working the same movement/muscles. As tri-sets can be quite demanding, it is a good idea to place a smaller muscle group movement or active stretch between A1 and A3. Let's look at an example in table 8.3.

This tri-set takes three distinctly different movement patterns and combines them. This raises the metabolic demand of the exercises and is not an approach well suited for maximal efforts. It is, however, an approach that can be used to target specific energy systems in the body and to develop strength endurance.

Table 8.3

Sequence	Exercise	Reps	Sets	Tempo	Rest
A1	DB deadlift	12–15	2	3010	30 sec
A2	Seated calf raise	12–15	2	3010	30 sec
A3	T-press-ups	12–15	2	2010	30 sec

An alternative approach is to use the tri-set as a giant set by targeting the same movement pattern with each exercise. Table 8.4 is an example of a giant set for the biceps.

You can also be creative with your sets and reps using the giant set format by targeting a wide range of training outcomes. This method is less likely to stimulate specific improvements in one system, but can be useful when training time is limited or you are simply aiming to maintain strength qualities. The example shown in table 8.5 is for knee dominant exercises and covers a range of different strength qualities.

Pre- and post-fatigue methods

Pre-fatiguing, also known as pre-exhaustion, is an approach best suited to muscle group orientated programmes. Pre-fatiguing involves performing an isolation exercise before a multi-joint exercise that uses the same muscles. This allows a muscle group to be worked to exhaustion during the main exercise. A good example of this is when performing the bench press, the arms may fatigue before the chest. In this case, a pre-fatigue exercise for the chest muscles before the bench press would overload them faster on the main exercise. Table 8.6 shows two examples of the pre-fatigue method.

On the other hand you may want to try to fatigue an accessory muscle in a lift first to stimulate extra development in that muscle as shown in table 8.7, targeting the biceps.

The obvious limitation to this system is that it will limit performance in the main exercise by intentionally weakening you first. However, this can be an effective way to overcome a

Table 8.4

Sequence	Exercise	Reps	Sets	Tempo	Rest
A1	EZ bar Scott curl	6–8	3	4210	minimal
A2	Sranding screw curls	8–10	3	3010	minimal
A3	Seated hammer curls	8–10	3	3010	90 sec

Table 8.5

Sequence	Exercise	Reps	Sets	Tempo	Rest
A1	Front squats	6	3	40X0	90 sec
A2	Bulgarian split squats	12	3	3020	90 sec
A3	Petersen step ups	20	3	2010	90 sec

Table 8.6

Sequence	Exercise	Reps	Sets	Tempo	Rest
A1	DB chest fly	10–12	3	2020	None
A2	Barbell bench press	6–8	3	4010	90 sec

Table 8.7

Sequence	Exercise	Reps	Sets	Tempo	Rest
A1	EZ bar Scott curl	10–12	3	2020	60 sec
A2	Supinated grip chin-ups	4–6	3	4010	120 sec

Table 8.8

Sequence	Exercise	Reps	Sets	Tempo	Rest
A1	Barbell overhead press	6–8	4	4010	60 sec
A2	DB scaptions	10–12	4	2020	120 sec

weak link, or to stimulate growth in a particular area.

The post-fatigue method is very similar, except in this case the isolation exercise is performed after the main complex movement. The idea behind this is to further the prime movers for the exercise that may not have been fully exhausted due to other areas fatiguing first. Table 8.8 is an example, where the performance of the elbow extensors has limited the fatigue in the shoulders. Hence an isolation movement for the shoulders is used to further exhaust them.

If you really are a glutton for punishment then you can always combine these methods to totally exhaust a certain body part, this effectively creates a giant set for a specific body-part. These methods are intense and should be used with care. Table 8.9 shows an example for the triceps.

Drop sets

There are a couple of versions of drop sets (also known as descending sets or strip sets), one of which is fairly well known and practised and another version that has similarities to cluster training and rest/pause, which is outlined later. Let's look at the first, more common type of drop set, which is a continuation of the post-fatigue approach to completely exhaust a movement or muscle group. Done correctly, this is an intense technique so use it sparingly.

The simple aim is to complete your last work set to technical failure (the point where you can no longer complete the exercise with totally perfect technical form), then to reduce the weight by around 10–15% (hence the term strip set, from stripping the bar of weight) and once again with minimal rest perform a set to failure, repeating the process for up to 6 additional sets.

Table 8.9

Sequence	Exercise	Reps	Sets	Tempo	Rest
A1	Tricep dips	10–12	3	4210	60 sec
A2	Dumbbell bench press	8–10	3	3010	60 sec
A3	Close grip press	AMRAP*	3	3010	120 sec

*AMRAP = as many repetitions as possible

To get the most from your drop set, two aspects are critical. Firstly, work to a point of technical failure on each set, so as soon as the target muscle is totally fatigued, reduce the weight and go again. Secondly, for this to be effective, use it with little or no rest between the drop sets.

The second version of the drop set is somewhat different. Begin the set with a maximal or near-maximal load and take only a short rest (10 seconds) between **each** repetition dropping the weight slightly each time. This can be hard work on your own so you will ideally need a partner to strip the weight for you after each rep. Working with the heavier weight means that this method can help build maximal strength levels and allow a greater average weight to be lifted over the course of a set. The short rest between each repetition also allows the high-threshold fast-twitch fibres to recover for the next rep.

In the example shown in table 8.10, there is a drop set for someone who can squat 150kg for 1RM. Between each rep the bar is momentarily racked, stripped, and then the next lift is performed.

As you can see, each repetition is effectively becoming a maximal, compared to a conventional 6RM set where only the final repetition would typically require maximal motor unit activation. Remember, the body will only use what it has to in order to complete a repetition, so the drop set format can create higher levels of muscular tension and effort with each repetition than simple continuous reps.

Pyramids

Pyramid type training has fallen out of favour over the years in place of performing more sets at the target weight. The name pyramid comes from the way that the load tapers in the same way a pyramid starts wide at the bottom and then narrows to the top.

Russian strength training authority Vladimir Zatsiorsky is scathing of it stating that it is 'ineffective and possibly detrimental' to strength development. The reason for this is that a typical pyramid format involves a lot of sub-maximal sets building up to the main work sets. A typical pyramid routine is shown in table 8.11 for bench presses.

In the past, it would be common to actually go back down the pyramid once the maximal lift has been performed. It isn't just the load that

Table 8.10			
Repetition	Load (Kg)	Tempo	Sets
I	150	40X0	10 secs
2	142.5	40X0	10 secs
3	135	40X0	10 secs
4	130	40X0	10 secs
5	125	40X0	10 secs
6	120	40X0	10 secs

Table 8.11			
Sets	Reps	Load	Rest
I	10	10RM	60 sec
2	8	8RM	60 sec
3	6	6RM	90 sec
4	4	4RM	120 sec
5	3	3RM	240 sec
6	2	2RM	240 sec
7	1	1RM	240 sec

can be pyramided; you can also apply a similar format to either the rest intervals or the repetition range. In fact, you can probably see some similarities to this method and the previously mentioned drop sets, which could be called reverse pyramids.

The major drawback with this type of pyramid is the intensity spread that it covers and the high volume of work performed before getting to the highest intensity lifts at around 1–2RM. This is only really likely to fatigue you early on before getting to the sets where you need to be at your freshest. However, other strength coaches are slower to dismiss the pyramid system altogether and suggest that an alternative would be to work over a far smaller range of intensity as in table 8.12, below.

Table 8.12			
Sets	Reps	Load	Rest
1	3	3RM	120 sec
2	2	2RM	180 sec
3	1	1RM	240 sec
4	1	1RM	240 sec
5	2	2RM	180 sec
6	3	3RM	120 sec

Wave loading

The reduced intensity spread pyramid leads nicely into a system of training known as wave loading, which has its roots in Bulgarian weightlifting in its purest form. This system uses a series of ascending waves designed to create greater excitement within the nervous system. There are many different versions of this, so in table 8.13 I have chosen a simple and practical version that you can apply to your

own training. I have used it successfully with several of my own clients to improve their strength.

Table 8.13		
Sets	Reps	Rest
1	5	120 sec
2	3	180 sec
3	2	180 sec
4	5	120 sec
5	3	180 sec
6	2	180 sec

The first shown is a wave-loading protocol for a relative strength session for an experienced lifter where you would begin the second wave with a slightly increased weight than that used in the first. A novice lifter aiming for strength would tend to work at a slightly lower intensity (such as a wave of 8, 6, and 4). Here there are two distinct waves, for a total of six sets. The strange neural effects of wave loading often result in an increase in strength on the second wave, with the previous attempts having greatly aroused the nervous system without creating undue fatigue. Let's look at an example for an advanced lifter interested in gaining muscle size (table 8.14).

Table 8.14

Sets	Reps	Rest
1	10	60 sec
2	8	60 sec
3	6	60 sec
4	10	60 sec
5	8	60 sec
6	6	60 sec

In this version we have introduced a higher rep range and shorter rest periods to focus the effort on stimulating muscle growth. Although this method can definitely add interest and variety to general training, it is at its best when training higher intensities at lower reps as it is more reliant on creating a neural effect rather than a metabolic one.

Contrast training

Contrast training is a great way to really add some variation to each and every set you do. As with the other methods we have discussed it can be done in a wide variety of ways. Some of these methods are more established than others and to add to the confusion this is often referred to as complex training. This can all get a little complicated, although the rationale behind this type of training is relatively simple. First, we need to briefly dive into the world of sports science and something called post-tetanic potentiation or PTP.

PTP is a fairly easy concept to understand – any muscular contraction leaves an after-effect and this effect can be used to generate greater levels of force in a subsequent contraction. So, the idea is fairly basic, firstly perform an intense muscular contraction (using near maximal weights), which will create a large PTP and then harness this effect by performing another exercise directly after.

Research has shown that this effect is at its most pronounced several minutes after the initial activity, further proof, if needed, of the central role the nervous system plays in strength development. The man credited with the idea of complex/contrast training is Russian Dr Yuri Verkhoshansky and his work has been adapted by many others in different formats although research is still a bit thin on the ground for its validity on the upper body and its crossover to sports performance.

So, let's take a look at some examples of contrast training supersets for improving explosive strength (tables 8.15 and 8.16). Training should combine bio-mechanically similar movements, although some research indicates that this need not always be the case as improvements have been seen when opposite movement patterns have been combined in a similar format.

Alternatively, it is sometimes preferred to perform the second exercise in the complex immediately after the first, which although it might be more metabolically taxing, is questionable for improving power. Complex training needn't only be performed as a superset either;

Table 8.15	Contrast superset for the lower body					
Sequence	Exercise	Reps	Load	Sets	Tempo	Rest
A1	BB front squats	3	85–95% of 1RM	4	4010	180 sec
A2	Jump squats	6	30–50% of 1RM	4	X0X0	180 sec

Table 8.16	Contrast for the upper body					
Sequence	Exercise	Reps	Load	Sets	Tempo	Rest
A1	Bench press	3	85–95% of 1RM	4	4010	180 sec
A2	Plyometric press-ups	10	30–50% of 1RM	4	X0X0	180 sec

Table 8.17	Contrast for the upper body					
Sequence	Exercise	Reps	Load	Sets	Tempo	Rest
A1	Front squats	3	85–95% of 1RM	1–3	4010	180 sec
A2	Cleans	5	85–95% of 1RM	1–3	30X0	180 sec
A3	Jump squats	10	40% 1RM	1–3	20X0	180 sec
A4	Depth jump	10	Bodyweight	1–3	X0X0	180 sec
A5	Vertical jumps	AMRAP in 15 secs	Bodyweight	1–3	X0X0	180 sec

you could build giant's sets ranging from high-intensity movements through to bodyweight ones, as shown in table 8.17 from coach Chris Thibaudeau.

The final version of contrast training that we will look at is the method of using contrasts within the same set of exercise. This is also known as mixed-tempo sets. With this method you ideally need a partner to help with altering the load of the bar, although it isn't essential.

With this type of training you can aim to build relative strength, explosive strength, hypertrophy, and strength endurance all within the confines of one set of work (repeated 3–5 times). Let's take a look at an example in table 8.18.

In this version, you can see that reps 1 and 2 are both relative strength focused with a slow lowering phase and pressing back as fast as possible (this may take 2–3 seconds so it is more practical to simply show an X as the weight can only be moved as fast as is possible). Reps 3, 4,

5 are all explosively performed using a lighter weight with a fast but controlled lowering and a high speed explosive concentric phase. Reps

Table 8.18		
Rep	Load	Tempo
1	3RM (~90% 1RM)	40X2
2	3RM (~90% 1RM)	40X2
3	60% of 1RM	10X0
4	60% of 1RM	10X0
5	60% of 1RM	10X0
6	60% of 1RM	3020 sec
7–12	60% of 1RM	3020 sec

6–12 use the same weight but at a different tempo, aiming for more time under tension for the muscle throughout the set to encourage a growth stimulus.

Note: throughout this section and the previous section several references have been made to attempting to move the weight as fast as possible on the concentric phase of the exercise and not letting the weight dictate the speed. For example, when performing contrast training the natural speed for moving a bar loaded at 60% will not be as quick compared to when a marked effort is made to move it at high speed. This is called compensatory acceleration training or CAT.

Hybrids and complexes training

Hybrids or sequence training is a great way to improve metabolic conditioning. Hence it has become a favoured method of the mixed martial arts fighter, as well as being a superior way to train when time is limited.

Hybrid training involves using a combination of exercises in sequence, either in the same repetition or in the same set. You can perform these using dumbbells, barbells, kettlebells, medicine balls, in fact just about anything you want. By combining exercises you get a true total body training effect that will boost metabolism and shift body fat rapidly. Let's take a look at some of these hybrids in action.

First up is the hybrid repetition, which is simply made by combining a minimum of two exercises. Your only limitation here is your imagination, as we will see.

Here are some straightforward two-exercise hybrids.
• Squat to overhead press
• Clean to front squat
• Deadlift to clean pull
• Dumbbell snatch to overhead squat (Ouch!)

Once you have the hang of picking two exercises to go together why stop there? Here is a particularly challenging complex that I like to use with a relatively light load for a warm-up before performing the Olympic lifts, although it can also work very well as a main workout on its own.
• Deadlift
• Romanian deadlift
• Clean pull
• Clean
• Front squat
• Overhead press
• Back squat
• Overhead press

Alternatively, you can try this one for another gut-busting complex either with a barbell, dumbbells, or even kettlebells!
• Deadlift
• Romanian deadlift
• Snatch
• Overhead squat
• Front squat

You can even try a single arm complex using either a dumbbell or a kettlebell.
• Single arm swings
• Single arm snatch
• Single arm overhead squat
• Single arm clean
• Single arm press

The obvious limitation of complexes is that you can only use a weight that you can lift for the weakest movement in the complex. For example, in the above complexes the weakest movement would be the overhead squat. So your deadlift would be comparatively easy. For this reason, use complexes when trying to develop total body high density strength/endurance.

Circuit training

For many years now circuit training has been the bastion of military and public service fitness routines. Simple to set-up, ideal for groups, and challenging in nature, circuit training is still a popular class in many health clubs despite not being as fashionable as many of the other concept classes. The multi-faceted nature of circuits mean that fairly modest improvements tend to be seen across a range of variables, rather than the more specific improvements seen in conventional resistance training methods.

Circuit training is essentially the same concept as applied to supersets – sequencing exercises with different focuses to make a more time efficient format. A typical circuit will often combine strength-based movements (squats, press-ups, dips) with more endurance-based exercises (step ups, jogging, squat thrusts, etc). It has proved to be effective in general conditioning for the recreational exerciser, and with careful planning can also be adapted for more specific outcomes. Research has shown that when matched for oxygen consumption circuits also have a higher metabolic cost (presumably due in large part to the amount of anaerobic energy metabolism involved) compared to aerobic modes such as running and cycling and therefore may be more effective when trying to improve body composition.

Problems come with circuits when considering technique. Firstly, the idea of racing against the clock to complete an exercise is not one likely to draw attention to correct technique and it is not uncommon to see some terrible attempts at performing exercise. Secondly, as fatigue increases posture and stability start to become compromised, which again leads to detrimental changes in exercise technique. A circuit should allow for adequate rest stations and simple exercises to mitigate these points. An example of a circuit approach is shown in the sample programmes for fat loss, Chapter 10.

Cluster training

Cluster training is brutally effective, but not to be overused as it combines high intensity work with a greater volume than would normally be the case when using continuous repetition methods. Again this makes a great method for shock cycles of training or for plateau busting. Cluster training is basically interval training for strength work, using short rest periods between each repetition to allow the high threshold motor fibres to recover before the next effort. This allows a greater volume of work to be achieved at a higher percentage of the 1RM. In table 8.19 below we show one set using a 3RM load with a 10–15 second rest between reps (heavier and more fast-twitch types will need nearer 15 than 10). This would be repeated for 5 sets.

Table 8.19			
Rep	Tempo	Load	Rest
1	401	3RM	10–15 sec
2	401	3RM	10–15 sec
3	401	3RM	10–15 sec
4	401	3RM	10–15 sec
5	401	3RM	10–15 sec

This method known as intensive clustering can really ramp up your workout volume. Lets look at the simple maths of the above system compared to performing the repetitions continuously.

We will assume a 3RM of 150kg on the bench press as an example. For 5 sets of 3 continuous reps, that would yield 15 (5 x 3) total reps totalling 2250kg of volume. In comparison, if you used the cluster training approach for 5 sets, it would yield a total of 25 reps (5 x 5) making a total volume of 3750kg, a difference of a staggering 1500kg!

Now let's look at how this method might be applied to training for muscle mass, where a greater length set is needed to stimulate muscle growth. In table 8.20 below we will perform an extensive cluster for the arms, assuming a 10RM of 50kg for the EZ bar curl.

Table 8.20			
Rep	Tempo	Load	Rest
1/2/3	3020	10RM	10–15 sec
4/5/6	3020	10RM	10–15 sec
7/8/9	3020	10RM	10–15 sec
10/11/12	3020	10RM	10–15 sec
13/14/15	3020	10RM	10–15 sec

In this case we are performing 3 reps in each cluster for a total of 15 reps; this would be done for 3 sets. Once again, this can be very effective, particularly for slow-twitch types, due to the extra volume of work performed. 10 reps at 50kg for 3 sets (30 total reps) totals 1500kg compared to the 2250kg possible with the cluster method a difference of 750kg for the exercise!

Remember, don't overdo it with this method. It is best used to break plateaux; too great an amount is very likely to lead to fatigue and overtraining.

A more common variation of cluster training is called rest/pause, which is simply any method of training that includes short pauses (typically 10–15 seconds) between reps, or at the end of a set, to allow partial recovery before resuming lifting. This is shown earlier in one format of drop sets.

German volume training

If you are interested in packing on some size and are not too concerned about training variety or finesse then GVT is most definitely the choice for you. GVT shot to fame in the mid 90s popularised by strength coach Charles Poliquint, and has since been seen in many different forms. It bears strong similarity to the 8 x 8 approach Vince Gironda advocated, instead using 10 sets of 10 reps on one exercise per movement pattern.

GVT is pretty simple and definitely brutal, with the theory being that you hit one movement pattern for 10 consecutive sets totally exhausting muscle fibres and stimulating a rapid response in size development. Let's take a look at an example of a GVT workout for a horizontal push and pull workout (table 8.21).

Now, while GVT will make you bigger, it probably won't make you stronger and you may even find you get weaker. It is also likely to make walking upstairs torturous for several days after doing 10 sets of squats. As part of a hypertrophy block you need a bit longer than for strength phases, so I would advise you to stick with it for up to six weeks before reverting to a strength phase. This sort of programme needs to be carefully used as the potential for overuse injuries is far greater with the repeated amounts of the same exercise.

5–10–20 or mixer routine

I found out about this training method from my father who used it in the early 80s as a great way to gain strength and size together. Another

Table 8.21					
Sequence	Exercise	Reps	Sets	Tempo	Rest
A1	DB bench press	10	10	3020	90 sec
A2	BB bent over row	10	10	3020	90 sec

variation on this is the 6–12–25 method used by Charles Poliquin. Both methods have a similar basis and a similar outcome. I call it the Mixer, as it combines heavy work with more traditional hypertrophy reps and muscle endurance, so you get a mix of high intensity with a good dose of volume.

Make sure for each set you pick a genuine 5, 10, and 20 rep max to get the most from this routine, and be warned it is tough. This will not only give you a great pump on the muscles you work, but will also send lactate levels rocketing – great for growth and fat loss.

Here is an example tri-set performed for a hip dominant split.

methods, however it has got some applications. In fact, sports such as gymnastics involve a high degree of isometric strength, consider the iron cross position on the rings as an example. An isometric contraction simply describes any exercise when the force is exerted without any visible change in muscle length and basically involves exerting a maximal effort against an immovable object, such as a racked and pinned bar or holding a weight in a set position. The practicalities of some isometric techniques can make the practice of them challenging; however, some interesting results have been seen when isometric training has been used, particularly regarding muscle hypertrophy responses.

Table 8.22					
Sequence	Exercise	Reps	Sets	Tempo	Rest
A1	Wide grip deadlift	5	3	4010	15 sec
A2	Dynamic lunge	10 each leg	3	3020	15 sec
A3	RDL	20	3		180 sec

Or try this version for the triceps

Table 8.23					
Sequence	Exercise	Reps	Sets	Tempo	Rest
A1	Barbell incline close grip press	5	3	4010	15 sec
A2	EZ bar French press	10	3	3020	15 sec
A3	Close grip press-up	20	3	1010	180 sec

A few words about isometric training

Isometric work doesn't get a lot of general attention and is hardly the most glamorous of training

The research on isometric training is hard to decipher as methodology and comparisons with other training modes (not to mention joint angle, sets, reps, volume, time of contraction, etc, all having a part to play) are confounding and often contradictory. However, specificity of training tells us that if we train isometrically, then the biggest effect is likely to be seen in isometric strength and at the exact point of the movement at which we train (though many texts cite anywhere between a 10–20 degree carryover of strength, dependant on joint angle). In fact the whole thing can become a bit confusing if you consider that the point in a movement where velocity drops to zero (such as when you hit a sticking point) is also effectively isometric training! This is a slower developing kind of muscle tension compared to one rapid explosion of effort against an immovable object and therefore is likely to produce a different training effect.

The pros of isometrics are mainly the joint specific angle you can train at (see one way to apply this below), the low energy cost, and the large amount of work performed at a maximal level. On the down side they can be highly hazardous for anyone with cardiovascular problems, are only specific to the angle trained, can be hard to measure in terms of progress or effort, may reduce range of movement, and can fatigue the nervous system quickly.

It is well worth experimenting with isometric training, although a complete breakdown of all the possible methods is beyond this book. However, here is a system using isometrics that you can try to help break through a troublesome sticking point on an exercise. Research has shown that you can make some impressive gains in 1RM using this technique.

- Set up a power rack with two pins in the training range. The top pin will be set at the exact point in the movement where you have the sticking point and the bottom pin at the bottom of the movement.
- Perform the lifting phase of the movement as normal until the bar contacts the top pins. They then continue to apply force against the bars gradually working up to a maximum effort.

- Hold this effort for up to 8 seconds, rest for 10 seconds and repeat for up to 6 repetitions. As a guide you should limit your time training with isometrics to 10–15 minutes a workout and rotate it through your training as you would any other methods.

Other methods

It goes without saying that there are many other methods of training with free weights that have not been outlined in this chapter, along with a multitude of training programmes – some of which are the same in practical terms just under a different name, others which are more suited to advanced and elite level lifters only. Dedicated plyometric training, for example, is used commonly to improve explosive strength and has only been given brief mention in this book, which is merely a reflection of the sheer depth of the topic. However, this selection represents enough material to keep you busy for some time and should serve as an introduction to the many choices for organising sets and reps. There is very little new in the strength training world and as we have already mentioned greater success comes from successfully rotating a small number of methods rather than constantly applying the latest workout from *Big Biceps Monthly*. As is continually stated, the perfect programme or exercise simply doesn't exist and there is little point wasting time looking for it in every source you read. Anyone promising it is likely more concerned with selling their latest product than seriously producing results.

Hopefully, you will now have some simple and easily implemented tools to add to your training toolbox. Now let's see how we can put them together on a more long-term basis to generate a periodised training programme.

Now we have looked at the basics of what makes a training programme and how to put together the various programme variables, let's take a look at more long-term planning, otherwise known as periodisation.

Periodising training can be a complicated topic littered with sports science terminology and complex formulas, although for those relatively new to weight training it needn't be so confusing. For the novice to weight training, more will be gained from focusing on sound technique and execution over complex programming approaches. As you become experienced, the need for periodised training becomes more apparent to allow for recovery and to facilitate progression. Further reading on periodisation is suggested in the bibliography.

Periodisation is the planned variation of different programme variables over regular intervals of time. It has been shown to bring about optimal gains in strength, fitness, power, motor performance, and hypertrophy compared to non-periodised methods.

Although research has clearly established the superiority of a periodised method over non-periodised, exactly how to go about it is a bit more controversial. By not using any kind of planned approach you are surely heading for a plateau in your training that will be frustrating and demotivating; not to mention the fact that doing the same stuff week in, week out, at the gym gets boring. There are many different things you can alter in a training programme in order to keep it varied. Some examples are as follows:

- Load
- Reps
- Sets
- Speed of movement
- Volume of work
- Rest periods
- Contraction types
- Frequency of training
- Choice of exercise
- Type of exercise/training method

You also need to think a bit laterally about your training. For example, if you are someone interested in getting bigger, you may be tempted to simply work on hypertrophy formats week after week. However, by learning to activate your fast-twitch motor fibres better in a relative strength block you can lift greater weights during a hypertrophy phase, potentially breaking down more proteins and stimulating greater size gains. This also allows your body to take a break from the high volume that is characteristic of muscle building type training approaches. Many of my clients have had noticeable improvements in their physiques having taken a break from working in the 8–12 repetition bracket and including some higher intensity strength work into their programme. In a similar way, if you are someone interested in Olympic lifting, your strength may be limiting your explosive ability and time might be better spent on developing your maximal strength through assistance lifts before returning to the Olympic movements. Here are some suggestions of areas you might want to work on.

- **Strength.** Based on using methods to increase relative and absolute strength through all movement patterns. This type of phase tends to involve more stable exercises that favour high-intensity loading such as squats, barbell presses, deadlifts, and rows.
- **Power.** Training for power involves all of the exercises that combine speed and strength. This can access a wide range of means, often combining them with developing better power production. It may be based around lightly loaded plyometric methods, or alternatively around heavier explosive lifts, such as the Olympic lifts.
- **Structure.** Structural training is principally aimed at developing or maintaining muscle and connective tissue. Sometimes called anatomical adaptation phases, these are the mainstay of the bodybuilder and will often include a larger element of isolation work at slower tempos than other phases. However, this phase can also be used to add muscle mass to an athlete or to prepare the body for a period of high intensity lifting that is to follow. In this phase in particular some strength and speed work should be included to prevent loss of power.
- **Metabolic.** Metabolic training focuses on a range of efforts including strength endurance and energy system development. This type of training can produce changes in more aerobic measures of fitness such as VO2 max and can target both anaerobic and aerobic systems through a variety of means. The most commonly used methods include circuit training, interval training, and metabolic resistance training with short-rest periods and whole-body movements.
- **Stability/functional.** These types of phases are growing in popularity in the sports world and everyday health enthusiast who may not be looking for specific system improvements. Often these trainees can be well-served

through a rotation of methods or a concurrent approach that focuses on a wide range of training means at the same time.

These five headings alone will largely dictate the direction of each training phase and will normally provide you with sufficient information on which to base their sets, reps, and other acute variables. Let's take a look at how we can start putting together our training blocks to make a longer term programme.

Periodisation of your workouts can be done in a couple of basic ways. We can either try to focus on improving one area of performance at a time and then linking these phases (sequenced training), or we can try to improve everything at the same time (concurrent training). If you train only once or twice a week, the second option is usually the best. If you are aiming for more specific improvements, or you compete in a sport, building a programme with blocks of training is a better option. If you train regularly (4 times per week +) you are better able to maintain your other strength qualities while working on one main focus for improvement, effectively blending the two strategies.

The most well-known model of periodisation is a simplified version of that first developed by the Russian Leonid Matveyev, which was based on an inverse link between intensity and volume with volume starting high and decreasing before competition as the intensity increased. Since then many models have been proposed, although the research still hasn't conclusively shown any one method to be superior to the other. The linear method first described by the Russians, then later adapted is shown overleaf (table 9.1) to illustrate the inverse relationship previously mentioned. This example gives no mention to intensity (as this will be highly subjective to change in the novice) or skills/technique training, it simply shows the basic structure. Each phase (also known as a mesocycle) would typically be 4–6 weeks in length and would be progressed by adding load to the exercise once the prescribed amount of sets/reps are successfully completed. Although this model has been heavily criticised, novices to weight training can make solid gains using this approach over a period of months without the need for further complexity.

Table 9.1

Phase	Sets	Reps
1	2	20
2	3	12
3	4	8
4	5	5

Another alternative is something called undulating (non-linear) periodisation, which research has shown to be very effective at improving overall strength, particularly over a shorter period of time (less than 12 weeks). The effectiveness of this system makes it an ideal choice for when time is short, such as in the athletic pre-season where the use of sequenced training blocks would be impractical. Undulating training programmes may change daily, weekly, or monthly depending on your needs, but as the principle behind them is the stimulus of the nervous system for strength gains, I favour a daily altering of training variables. As these systems are better suited to experienced lifters, they are sometimes shown in terms of sets/reps relationships or more simply as varied levels of intensity. As this method exposes you to high-intensity lifting from the start it is wise to precede this with a period of linear periodisation if you are new to weight training.

Here is an example of undulating periodisation that you can use with a whole-body workout.

Table 9.2

Day	Intensity	Sets/Reps
Monday	Moderate	4 × 8
Wednesday	Light	2 × 12
Friday	High	6 × 4

Here is another example, this time using a four-day training split.

Table 9.3

Day	Intensity	Sets/Reps
Monday	High	8 × 3
Tuesday	Moderate	3 × 10
Thursday	Light	2 × 15
Friday	High (speed)	10 × 2

You can probably see how this can all get a bit confusing, although what it comes down to is that regular changes in programming are important for progress. When total training volume is the same, research has shown making daily changes in intensity to be more effective than making changes every 4-6 weeks. This can be achieved through altering many of the different training variables.

What is better established is that the more advanced the lifter, the more complex their training approach needs to be, and more importance is given to the cumulative effect of the workouts.

Building blocks of training

We have seen in the previous section that we have the option to alter our exercise variables on either a daily, weekly, or monthly basis. This can be achieved using either a linear approach that keeps training variables fairly constant over a block or phase of training and using progressive increases in resistance, or by using an undulating approach that changes sets, reps, tempo, and load on a more frequent basis. So, how can we put this together to make a more long-term plan for our training?

I favour the simple approach of building blocks of training. Each block has a particular emphasis or training focus, but is not exclusive to that focus – instead including elements of each requisite strength quality required by that one person.

Training blocks for most will last 4–6 weeks. As a rule of thumb, when working on structural changes I favour longer blocks, and when concentrating on neural adaptations, I prefer shorter blocks to shock the body into change.

Each block ends with a week of reduced volume to allow for recovery and adaptation. This is simply done by reducing the amount of sets performed in that week by around 40%. Let's have a look at an example of a couple of blocks.

Firstly here is a four-week block designed to improve power.

Table 9.4

Week	Training method	Sets/Reps
1	Supersets	4 × 4–6
2	Contrast	3 × 6, 3 × 10
3	Contrast	3 × 6, 3 × 10
4	Recovery	2 × 6

The above block has used a lower-volume week initially, before two hard weeks of contrast training (see Chapter 8) and then finishing with a recovery week to allow for adaptation to the shock cycle. Similarly, the following example uses wave loading over two weeks after an introductory week to try and improve relative strength levels.

Table 9.5

Week	Training method	Sets/Reps
1	Supersets	4 × 4–6
2	Wave loading	4/2/1 4/2/1
3	Wave loading	4/2/1 4/2/1
4	Supersets	3 × 6

Let's have a look at another block, this time a structural block, aimed at increasing muscle mass.

Table 9.6

Week	Training method	Sets/Reps
1	Supersets	3 × 10
2	Pre-fatigue	3 × 10, 3 × 8
3	Pre-fatigue	3 × 10, 3 × 8
4	Pre-fatigue	3 × 10, 3 × 8
5	Supersets	3 × 10

This block is slightly longer to allow for anatomical adaptations, which happen slower than neural changes. It uses a high volume of load and pre-fatigue techniques to stimulate increased protein breakdown and muscle hypertrophy.

Of course, the permutations for structuring your training blocks are almost without limit, although my advice is to keep it simple to start with. The more advanced the athlete, the more advanced and long-term planning will be required to keep adaptations happening. Here are some suggestions on how to join your training blocks together to make a plan for a year or

6 month period (also known as the training macrocycle).

To put together a set of training blocks you need three key pieces of information.

Where am I now?

Where do I want to be?

What do I need to do to get from 1 to 2?

Obviously, if it was that simple then I wouldn't have a job or need to write this book, but it is a fairly simple principle. You just have to look at your training and decide what it is you need it to do for you. The more specific your needs are, the more specific your training must be. Conversely if you have fairly generic and broad goals, then your training can reflect that. Lets take a look at a range of block progressions for various different types of trainee.

As you can see, this is far from rocket science. Some might argue that it is overly simple, although this degree of programme planning is already several levels above that of many trainees. The blocks are rotated to emphasise the most important qualities to that individual. Therefore, a bodybuilder will spend more time on hypertrophy, a quality that would be detrimental to the performance of an aerobic distance athlete, who would be better strengthening their stabilisers and improving strength endurance of postural muscles. In contrast, the Olympic lifter devotes more time to improving their explosive power, with a regular return back to working on their relative strength levels.

Obviously, you can take the concept of periodisation to a far more scientific level than

Table 9.7	Progression for novice trainee		
Stability	Structure	Strength	Power

Table 9.8	Progression for gaining muscle/bodybuilding				
Hypertrophy	Strength	Hypertrophy	Hypertrophy	Strength	Hypertrophy

Table 9.9	Progression for power athlete/Olympic lifting				
Hypertrophy	Strength	Power	Strength	Power	Power

Table 9.10	Progression for strength athlete				
Hypertrophy	Strength	Strength	Power	Strength	Strength

Table 9.11	Progression for aerobic athlete (distance runner)				
Stability	Metabolic	Stability	Strength	Stability	Metabolic

Table 9.12	Progression for anaerobic/aerobic athlete (rugby)				
Metabolic	Strength	Power	Metabolic	Strength	Power

we have here, although I do believe that this approach is simple enough to require little effort to even the most casual of trainee. Now all you have to do is sit down and write out your own blocks and you are ready to go!

Remember that just because you are focusing on hypertrophy during a block of training, it is not wise to completely neglect other methods – such as speed/strength work, which tends to disappear quickly if untrained. The adage here is use it, or lose it. To ensure you maintain all your strength qualities, use a small amount of each during each phase to retain their level.

Getting over a training plateau

We all get stuck sometimes but it need not be the end of the world and usually can be sorted out with a bit of simple adjustment. Here are some simple tips you can try if you have found things starting to stagnate.

- **Take a break.** Many people who lift weights regularly are in a constant state of overtraining and sometimes all you need to get an improvement is a break to let the body recover and adapt. Try reducing your volume by 40–50% for a week while maintaining the intensity levels to allow some recovery.
- **Change your technique.** Simply by varying grip width, foot position, stance type, or range of movement you alter the neural demand of the exercise and this is often enough to prompt a change in performance.
- **Use a shock method.** The opposite to taking a break is to employ a week of shock tactics where you use a particularly brutal training approach (such as heavy cluster training) to shock the body into progress. It is important to follow this with a recovery week.
- **Check your structural balance.** More often than not this means some work on those forgotten areas such as the rotator cuff. Some areas can start to fall behind when not maximally stressed in training. By improving those areas you can get the body working as one unit again.
- **Use small incremental weight increases.** Sometimes the increase in weight available with a standard plate is one step too far. Smaller increases such as 0.25kg or 0.5kg can be added through fractional weight plates to make the step up in weight less severe.
- **Change your warm-up.** It may be that your warm up is either too demanding and long, or too brief. Give this some thought before coming up with a different approach.
- **Change the sequence of exercises.** Altering the sequence of exercises in a workout can make a significant difference. Remembering to always keep your most complex and explosive lifts at the start of the workout, you still have plenty of latitude to move things around. It may well be that a fatiguing grip is your problem and a simple change in order may help with that.
- **Strengthen weak links.** It can sometimes be hard to identify these in the novice lifter although if there is a particular pattern of movement you struggle with then it can help to strengthen the individual links in that chain separately as well as together. A simple example is how strengthening the biceps and brachialis can help improve chin-up strength, or how improving lower back strength can build your deadlift.
- **Imbalance programmes deliberately.** If you know what you are doing then imbalancing a programme in favour of a particular movement or exercise can really help. If your quads are weak and squatting poor, doing it on the last workout of the week is not likely to help. Put your weakest movements first in any programme.

- **Take shorter, more frequent workouts.** Too long in one go can overly tax the nervous system and reduce strength. Beat this by training for less time, but more often.
- **Use specialist methods.** Simple examples include partial range training or isometrics, where you can strengthen specific parts of a set movement.
- **Change your programme more often.** If you have a highly efficient nervous system and learn fast, you are going to need regular changes in what you do. You can even change it every single time in some cases.
- **Leave it and come back to it.** Why not just leave the lift alone for 2–3 weeks and come back to it fully recovered?

How to split your training programme

The final thing to cover when designing your training programme is the ongoing debate over how to split your workouts. Should you train lower body/upper body? Perhaps use a body-part split? What about a movement pattern split or maybe stick to whole-body workouts instead?

My take on this situation is to choose the method most appropriate for you. Our individuality is the biggest factor in deciding the best way for each of us to train. This isn't just down to our individual physiology or biomechanics either, but also our training goals, frequency, diet, lifestyle, stress, and everything else. We must also be realistic about what can be achieved in the given time we have to train.

It is for this reason that whole-body training programmes are so beneficial for anyone training for all-round health and fitness. Similarly for the sportsperson who is using resistance training as supplementary work to their main sport, whole body or an upper/lower body split tends to be better.

Given that body-part split training has its origins in bodybuilding, it is difficult to say if there is a place for it amongst sports conditioning or general health training. Typically composed of a greater number of isolation exercises, body-part training fails to take account of many important aspects of weight training and can lead to imbalances in posture and muscle length if not carefully monitored for volume and movement dominance. A common example of this is working a chest programme one day (presses and flyes), followed by a back programme (lat pull-downs and chin-ups) later in the week. Although these days might have differences in terms of prime-movers, both are heavily reliant on the internal rotators of the shoulder. This type of programme, if not sufficiently varied can quickly lead to problems with shoulder imbalance and injury.

In general I do tend to favour whole body workouts for several reasons.

- Greater overall muscle mass used per workout
- Hits everything with each exposure
- Higher levels of energy needed per workout
- Greater cardiovascular stimulation
- Greater hormonal response
- Avoids high levels of soreness that can limit sports performance
- Greater total work accomplished per workout
- Simple for classification purposes

Body part training tends to sway programmes towards isolation exercises and away from whole body movements such as deadlifts, cleans, snatches, jerks, and their derivatives (such as hybrid movements and complexes). After all is a clean a shoulder exercise, arm exercise, hip exercise, or even a core exercise? Zatsiorsky states in his classic text *The Science and Practice of Strength Training* that, 'the entire movement pattern, rather than the strength of single muscles or the movement of a single joint, must be the primary training objective'. He is right because that is how the human body works. In reality we never simply work the biceps or the quads. Our brain thinks not in terms of individual muscles but rather movements. Locking the body into machines that fix joints in an unnatural way in an attempt to isolate one is largely a misguided practice that was never designed to actually improve performance or function.

So, what should you pick? Well, why pick just one method? It is relatively simple to combine a whole body approach with a slant towards strengthening certain body parts. For example, someone with weak elbow flexors may want to include some direct bicep work after having done chin ups with the plan that the extra volume on the weakest area will stimulate it to a greater degree. Similarly, it is wise to strengthen the lower back before attempting squats or deadlifts.

Much the same as selecting a periodisation scheme, or a specific pattern of sets/reps, this comes down to individual preferences. In general I would say that far too many people are using body part splits when they may achieve greater gains from a whole-body approach. Here are some examples of splits for 2, 3 and 4 day a week training programmes.

Twice a week

If you plan to train twice a week, you should train your whole body leaving a couple of days between workouts.

Table 9.13	
Day	**Split**
Monday	Whole body
Thursday	Whole body

Alternatively you can employ an upper/lower body split.

Table 9.14	
Day	**Split**
Tuesday	Upper body
Friday	Lower body

Three times a week

Training three times really opens up your options. Training can be split into movement patterns, body parts, upper/lower body, or simply kept as a whole body workout as shown below.

Table 9.15	
Day	**Split**
Monday	Whole body
Wednesday	Whole body
Friday	Whole body

Table 9.16	
Day	**Split**
Tuesday	Lower body
Thursday	Upper body
Saturday	Lower body

Simply alternate workout split week to week, so the following week would include two upper body and only one lower body workouts.

Table 9.17

Day	Split
Monday	Quad dominant and horizontal pull
Wednesday	Vertical push and vertical pull
Friday	Hip dominant and horizontal push

This workout uses movement pattern splits – abdominal and supplemental work can be added in as needed.

Table 9.18

Day	Split
Tuesday	Quad, hamstrings, calves
Thursday	Chest, biceps, abdominal
Saturday	Back, shoulders, triceps

This type of workout is seen less commonly now and is based around splitting muscle groups to train.

Table 9.19

Day	Split
Tuesday	Snatches and assistance lifts
Thursday	Jerks and assistance lifts
Saturday	Cleans and assistance lifts

This is a simple approach for those who base their training around the Olympic lifts, although many choose to perform each lift on every day.

Four Days a Week

For those with the time to train four times a week, this is possibly the ideal frequency as it allows for all kinds of combinations when splitting your training. Here are a few examples of how you might do it.

Table 9.20

Day	Split
Monday	Lower body
Tuesday	Upper body
Thursday	Lower body
Saturday	Upper body

Table 9.21

Day	Split
Monday	Squats and pushes
Tuesday	Lifts and pulls
Thursday	Squats and pushes
Saturday	Pulling/supplemental

Table 9.21 shows a split more suited to an explosive strength athlete – focusing on the big strength exercises.

Table 9.22

Day	Split
Monday	Hip dominant and calves
Wednesday	Horizontal push/pull
Friday	Quad dominant and abs
Sunday	Vertical push/pull

Table 9.23

Day	Split
Monday	Quad dominant and pulls
Tuesday	Hip dominant and pushes
Thursday	Quad dominant and pulls
Saturday	Hip dominant and pushes

Variations between days can be achieved using a blend of single leg and single arm exercises on alternate days.

Table 9.24

Day	Split
Monday	Chest and glute/hams
Tuesday	Back and shoulders
Thursday	Quads and calves
Friday	Arms and abdominals

This again is a bodybuilding type split oriented around muscles over movements.

Summary

Programme design really does form the nuts and bolts of your work in the gym. It has evolved into quite a precise science with many established textbooks and many ongoing debates about what works best for whom and where. However, for most of you reading this book programme design can be a relatively simple process that can still yield impressive differences in results compared to those training without purpose or direction. For anyone who wants more than just a better level of fitness, it is an integral part of your success.

Remember that the principle used here is that if you change nothing in your programme, then you should expect nothing to change in your performance.

By now you should feel armed with all the necessary tools to sit down and write yourself a weight training programme that covers all the basics such as sets and reps, through to your weekly training split and even your monthly training focus.

However, I am sure that there are a few of you who are keen to get started as soon as possible so I have included some basic workouts that will give you a range of different options along with some tips for how to design your own workouts for that goal. You should find it relatively easy to tweak these programmes to fit your own training needs.

Sample workout for fat loss

For people seeking fat loss, metabolic weight training is the prime method. Not only does weight training burn calories and improve all-round muscle tone, it also helps to increase the metabolism and improve strength. It should be your number one choice for improving body composition and stacks up far better than the usual favourite of doing endless aerobic exercise.

I use peripheral heart action (PHA) techniques for fat loss workouts, this method simply involves alternating between lower and upper body with each exercise in a circuit format. This raises lactate levels, which in turn promotes the release of a growth hormone that leads to fat burning. Tables 10.1 and 10.2 show an example of this.

It is easy to put together your own PHA type of workout by simply alternating between a lower body and upper body workout, be sure to use a balanced range of movements as discussed earlier in this book. Here is an example of how to design your own two-part

Table 10.1	Days 1 and 3				
Order	Exercise	Sets	Reps	Tempo	Rest
A1	Dumbbell swings	3	12–15	20X0	30
A2	Press-ups	3	12–15	3010	30
A3	Dumbbell split squats	3	12–15	4010	30
A4	Bent over rows (neutral grip)	3 3	12–15 12–15	3010	30
A5	Bar rollouts	3	12–15	3020	30
A6	Row 300m or sprint on bike	3	1 min	n/a	30

Table 10.2	Days 2 and 4					
Order	Exercise	Sets	Reps	Tempo	Rest
A1	Reverse lunges	3	12–15	20X0	30
A2	Inverted rows	3	12–15	3010	30
A3	Alternating arm snatches	3	12–15	4010	30
A4	Push press	3	12–15	3010	30
A5	Back extensions	3	12–15	3020	30
A6	Skipping	3	1 min	n/a	30

split. You can do this workout up to 4 times a week, simply alternate the two routines.

Circuit 1
A1   Hip dominant (double leg)
A2   Horizontal push
A3   Quad dominant (single leg)
A4   Horizontal pull
A5   Abdominals/twist
A6   High intensity cardio

Circuit 2
A1   Quad dominant (double leg)
A2   Vertical pull
A3   Hip dominant (single leg)
A4   Vertical push
A5   Abdominals/twist
A6   High intensity cardio

You can get further variety by experimenting with different intensity levels for the exercises although it is best to stick between 10–15 as this generates high levels of lactate, stimulating growth hormone production and fat loss. If you are looking to shift body fat through weight training then follow my five rules below.

1. Stick to compound movements. Compound movements use more muscle and therefore generate more lactate and a greater hormonal response.

2. Do everything standing and stay off machines. Most people sit down all day anyway, you are stronger when you are standing and you recruit more muscle when you are not on machines.

3. Combine movements and use hybrids for maximal muscle activation. This is all about density and means you get more work for the time spent, firing up your metabolism even more.

4. Use interval-based formats at higher intensities vs. low-intensity steady state training to stimulate fat burning enzyme changes in the body. Research has clearly shown the superiority of this approach for long-term fat burning. One study by the energy balance specialist, Tremblay, and his colleagues in 1994 showed a nine-fold increase in fat loss despite a much lower overall caloric expenditure *during* the sessions when using short burst intervals over longer aerobic endurance oriented protocols. Remember, it is how much fat you burn 24/7 that really counts, not just what you use in a workout. Higher intensity work has been shown to have a far greater effect on boosting your metabolism, not to mention being quicker and a more efficient way to train.

5. Include some heavier lifting and explosive work at the start of the session or on a separate day. I am a big believer in including higher intensity lifts in a fat loss programme, as it is essential to stimulate the higher threshold motor units, maintain strength and muscle mass, and to improve resting tone of muscles. Doing light weights or very high repetition sets (over 15) to get lean is a physiological oxymoron.

Sample training for muscle gain

We have already covered some of the methods at your disposal for muscle gain, such as German volume training or pre-/post-fatigue approaches. Here is an example of several different workouts that you could use if your goal is to increase size.

Tables 10.3 and 10.4 show a two-day programme, which is simply split into an upper body and lower body routine. This is an ideal routine for someone just getting started with weight training or bodybuilding. Those who have been following a similar routine for a while will want to start including methods such as drop sets, pre/post fatigue, hypertrophy clusters, or German volume training to get further results.

The German volume training approach mentioned earlier is a tough routine that is likely to leave you feeling fairly sore for a few

Table 10.3	Upper body				
Order	Exercise	Sets	Reps	Tempo	Rest
A1	Bent over row	3	10–12	3020	60
A2	Dumbbell bench press	3	10–12	3020	60
B1	DB upright row to sternum	3	10–12	2010	60
B2	Seated military press	3	10–12	3010	60
C1	EZ bar preacher curl	3	10–12	3020	45
C2	Tricep extensions	3	10–12	3020	45

Table 10.4	Lower body				
Order	Exercise	Sets	Reps	Tempo	Rest
A1	Deadlifts	3	10–12	3020	60
A2	Bulgarian split squats	3	10–12	3020	60
B1	Good mornings	3	10–12	2010	60
B2	Font squat	3	10–12	2010	60
C1	Straight leg calf raise	3	10–12	3020	45
C2	Bar rollouts	3	10–12	3020	45

days. Tables 10.5, 10.6 and 10.7 illustrate a high volume routine so ensure you get the most from it by taking in a good quality post-workout meal or supplement. Start with a weight around your 20RM and once you can complete 10 x 10 with it, increase it by around 5%.

Dedicated training days for arms are best left to the serious bodybuilders, but if you are keen to bring up their size then a couple of simple tri-sets can be added in at the end of a workout to boost the biceps and triceps (see tables 10.8 and 10.9). You can either alternate the tri-sets on different days or if time permits perform them together, perhaps on a day devoted to supplemental training exercises, dedicated core work, or flexibility training. Remember, the arms need plenty of variety so to keep them growing, you'll need to change this workout regularly.

Table 10.5	Knee dominant/vertical pull				
Order	Exercise	Sets	Reps	Tempo	Rest
A1	Barbell squat	10	10	4010	90
A2	Chin-ups	10	10	4010	90
B1	EZ bar curls	3	8–10	3020	60
B2	Seated incline hammer curls	3	8–10	3020	60

Table 10.6	Hip dominant/vertical push				
Order	Exercise	Sets	Reps	Tempo	Rest
A1	Barbell deadlift	10	10	4010	90
A2	Military press	10	10	4010	90
B1	Dips	3	8–10	3020	60
B2	Skullcrushers	3	8–10	3020	60

Table 10.7	Horizontal push/horizontal pull				
Order	Exercise	Sets	Reps	Tempo	Rest
A1	Dumbbell bench press	10	10	4010	90
A2	Bent over row	10	10	4010	90
B1	Weighted crunch	2	10–12	3020	45
B2	Back extension	2	10–12	4020	45
B3	External dumbbell rotation	2	10–12	4010	45

Table 10.8	Biceps				
Order	Exercise	Sets	Reps	Tempo	Rest
A1	Standing straight bar bicep curl	3	4–6	50X0	30 sec
A2	Seated incline hammer curls	3	8–10	3020	30 sec
A3	Preachers curls EZ bar 1/4 reps	3	AMRAP	4040	120 sec

Table 10.9	Triceps				
Order	Exercise	Sets	Reps	Tempo	Rest
A1	Close grip press	3	4–6	50X0	30 sec
A2	EZ bar skullcrushers	3	8–10	3020	30 sec
A3	Overhead dumbbell extension	3	12–15	2020	120 sec

There are many different approaches you can take to gain muscle, to help out here are my five rules for your muscle gain programmes.

1. Control your tempo – particularly the eccentric phase. So many people neglect the lowering phase of the exercise as they don't realise the impact that it can have on muscle growth. To maximise the breakdown of proteins within the muscle that leads to hypertrophy you must lower the weight slowly and under control.

2. Combine whole-body movements with isolation exercises. Not only are isolation exercises good for bringing up the weaker links in the chain, they are also an ideal tool for pre/post fatigue training or selectively targeting a lagging area. If your goal is to lift weight for size then they will likely be part of your routine.

3. Include some heavier lifting. Once again the importance of lifting heavier weights as part of your training crops up, particularly for women who can really see sufficient benefits. Lifting heavier weights makes you better able to activate muscle so you will be able to lift heavier loads when you return to your repeated effort work, leading to greater protein breakdown and increased gains.

4. Tension is key. High levels of muscular tension are central to muscle growth. This can be achieved through either tempo (Charles Poliquin recommends between 40–70 seconds per set for hypertrophy), increased load, or by consciously accelerating the load through the concentric phase of the movement. This is called compensatory acceleration training (CAT).

5. Change workouts every 4–6 exposures. Variety is important, but less so when working on anatomical adaptation as the stress is spread more evenly between the metabolic, musculoskeletal, and neural systems.

In hypertrophy training variation tends to be got through changes in exercises more than anything else.

Sample workouts for strength gains

At some point you will want to get into lifting at higher intensities, the examples shown here are basic programmes to introduce you to some heavier lifting. More advanced lifters will want to consider using methods such as contrast training, drop sets, cluster training, and wave loading to maintain a high level of neural stimulation. Strength routines feature less exercises and instead rely on getting variety through sets, reps, tempo, and periodisation approaches.

The first example shown is a whole-body routine that can be done twice per week for 3–4 weeks.

Table 10.10	Day 1				
Order	Exercise	Sets	Reps	Tempo	Rest
A1	Barbell good mornings	4	4–6	3010	90
A2	Military press	4	4–6	3010	90
B1	Back squat	4	4–6	40X0	90
B2	Chin-ups	4	4–6	3010	90
C1	Weighted crunch on stability ball	2	12–15	2010	60
C2	Dumbbell Cuban press	2	12–15	2010	60

Table 10.11	Day 2				
Order	Exercise	Sets	Reps	Tempo	Rest
A1	Stiff leg deadlifts	4	4–6	30X0	90
A2	Close grip incline press	4	4–6	4010	90
B1	Front squat	4	4–6	40X0	90
B2	Bent over rows	4	4–6	3010	90
C1	Glute ham raises	2	6–8	3010	60
C2	Dumbbell external rotations	2	10–12	40X0	60

The next example is using a three-day split and includes a wave loading protocol for the first two exercises.

Table 10.12	Day 1. Hip dominant and vertical push				
Order	Exercise	Sets	Reps	Tempo	Rest
A1	Barbell deadlifts	6	5/3/2/5/3/2	42X0	120
A2	Seated military press	6	5/3/2/5/3/2	4010	120
B1	Reverse grip RDL	3	4–6	40X1	90
B2	Dumbbell push press	3	4–6	4010	90

Table 10.13	Day 2. Horizontal pull/horizontal push				
Order	Exercise	Sets	Reps	Tempo	Rest
A1	Bent over barbell row	6	5/3/2/5/3/2	3010	120
A2	BB incline press	6	5/3/2/5/3/2	4010	120
B1	Single arm dumbbell row	3	4–6	4010	90
B2	Close grip becnch press	3	4–6	40X0	90

Table 10.14	Day 3. Knee dominant/vertical pull				
Order	Exercise	Sets	Reps	Tempo	Rest
A1	Barbell front squat	6	5/3/2/5/3/2	4012	120
A2	Wide grip chin-up	6	5/3/2/5/3/2	4010	120
B1	Barbell lunge	3	4–6	4010	90
B2	Close grip pull-ups	3	4–6	4010	90

These two examples should get your programming for strength gains off to a good start. To help you further here are my five tips for improving your strength performance.

1. High threshold fibre recruitment is key. To get stronger and more powerful you need to tap into the fast-twitch motor units, which means using heavy weights and moving them as quickly as possible.

2. Keep it below 6 reps when working on strength. Using lower reps leads to minimal protein breakdown in the muscle and therefore minimal muscle gain. This is ideal for sportspeople where competitors are assigned weight classes for their event.

3. Keep to whole-body multi-joint exercises. There is little place for isolation-type exercises in a relative strength programme as they are better suited to higher repetition routines.

4. Intent determines adaptation. Common belief is that lifting heavy weights makes you slow, which is simply not true. The key is to focus on trying to move the weight as fast as possible as it is the brain's intention to do this that dictates the adaptation to the exercise, rather than the actual speed itself.

5. Don't overuse methods. Recovery is paramount and this should be planned in. Methods such as wave loading should not be used week in, week out on every exercise, so apply them with discretion to achieve the best results.

Combinations

Once you have got the hang of the various aspects of designing your workout, you can start to design workouts that involve a number of different training aims. This type of approach is ideal for the more experienced weight trainee who might only lift weights once or twice a week as it allows you to maintain and even improve performance in a range of training variables. Check out the example below for a two-day whole-body programme that tackles power, speed, strength, and muscle gain.

Table 10.15	Day 1					
Order	Exercise	Sets	Reps	Tempo	Rest
A	Hang snatch	3	6/4/2	X0X0	120
B1	Deadlift	4	4–6	30X0	90
B2	Incline bench press	4	4–6	4010	90
C1	Single leg deadlift	2	10–12	3020	60
C2	Neutral grip overhead press	2	10–12	3020	60
D	External rotators	2	12–15	3020	60

Table 10.16	Day 2				
Order	Exercise	Sets	Reps	Tempo	Rest
A	Hang clean	3	6/4/2	X0X0	120
B1	Front squat	4	4–6	4010	120
B2	Chin-ups	4	4–6	4010	90
C1	Split stance squat 1½ Reps*	2	10–12	3020	60
C2	Inverted Rows	2	10–12	3010	60
D	Lower Trap Lifts	2	12–15	4010	60

* Go all the way down, come back up halfway, go back down then come up the whole way. This greatly increases muscular tension and promotes muscle growth.

Other methods

Energy system training

You will often read of the need to include 30–45 minutes of aerobic training into your fitness routine for 3–4 workouts a week. It is in fact very easy to improve your anaerobic and aerobic fitness using weights. Weight training can help to improve lactate tolerance, build local muscle endurance, and raise heart rate in a way most would struggle to achieve through conventional aerobic training equipment.

The best way to achieve aerobic fitness improvement with weights is to use interval based routines that combine dynamic whole body movements with callisthenics, sprinting, rowing, and low-intensity plyometrics. There are many ways to do this, for example, try combining a weight training exercise with a bodyweight aerobic-type exercise.

A1 Squat to press
A2 Skipping 1 minute
B1 Deadlifts to sternum pulls
B2 Skipping 1 minute

You can then either repeat a combination of exercises or perform a selected number or exercises in sequence. This simple way of training keeps each routine varied and enjoyable as well as simple and light on equipment.

Training to time

Another popular and easy to use system of training the energy systems is simply to train to time. This format is not as strictly structured around sets and reps as most of the other strength training methods and is ideal for those who may be motivated by working to the clock, or for group exercise. Put simply, set yourself a target amount of reps to achieve and try to do it as quickly as possible. Here are a couple of simple examples.

10 squats – 10 push-ups – 5 pull-ups.
Perform this on the minute, rest for what is left of the minute and go again. Aim to keep going for 20 minutes.

Cleans – front squats – push press.
Perform 5 reps of this complex on the minute,

rest for what is left of the minute and go again. Start with 5 rounds.

The 100. Choose an exercise and do 100 reps as quickly as possible. This is a great workout finisher using a bodyweight movement such as a squat. Alternatively, pick two strength exercises and work them back-to-back up to 100 reps for a seriously tough workout. Next time you do it aim to beat your time from before. As a workout finisher you can also perform some farmers' walks – simply grab a pair of heavy dumbbells and walk up and down the gym for a desired distance. This is a great way to build grip strength at the end of a workout.

There are many different variations on a theme and you are only limited by your imagination. This type of training is based on density and therefore tends to be an effective way to shift body fat and build muscular endurance.

Tabata training

Physiologist Izumi Tabata found that by using very short intervals of high intensity work on a stationary bike, combined with even shorter rest periods, it was possible to make significant gains in fitness in a very short space of time.

However, what was really interesting was that not only were there significant improvements in the anaerobic fitness of participants, but also in their aerobic fitness as well. This format is now widely used either for when time is tight in the gym, or when you want to condition people whose sport involves short periods of high intensity activity.

Here's how it works, slightly adapted for weight training. Select two exercises that are whole body movements. Perform exercise A1 for 20 seconds, rest for 10 seconds and then perform A2 for 20 seconds. Do this for a total of 8 intervals. Let's look at an example.

A1 Squat to dynamic overhead press for 20 seconds (performed as fast as possible). Rest 10 seconds.
A2 Kettlebell/dumbbell swings for 20 seconds. Rest 10 seconds and go back to A1 and repeat for 4 minutes.

Here is another example using bodyweight exercises only.
A1 Press-ups – 20 seconds. Rest 10 seconds.
A2 Jump squats – 20 seconds. Repeat for 4 minutes.

Try this and you will be surprised at just how hard 4 minutes of exercise can actually be. Use your imagination to come up with different combinations of exercises.

Summary

By now you have everything you need to get started on a programme of training with free weights. As long as you remember the basics of the acute exercise variables and how to best manipulate them for your chosen need, then you won't go far wrong.

These sample routines are intended to get you started but are a long way from complete training programmes. It is worth remembering that there is no such thing as the perfect programme, so you will need to experiment with a range of different exercises to find what works for you best.

This is by no means an exhaustive list of methods either, many of which are suited only to the advanced lifter or more specialised trainee, such as those interested only in Olympic lifting or powerlifting; further reading on these topics is shown in the bibliography.

It can also be difficult in the modern health club to use more complex methods, many don't have the equipment or set-up. It can also be a challenge during peak times in your local gym to even work on supersets when every time you turn your back someone throws their towel on the squat rack in preparation for ten sets of bicep curls. To avoid this problem, try to pair exercises so that you can don't have to leave the area you are working in. This is one of the great benefits that training with dumbbells and kettlebells offers over machines.

For those of you for whom time is tight and are looking for a quicker option than the above programmes, I recommend you use the complexes such as those shown in Chapter 8, which enable quick but highly demanding workouts.

CLOSING THOUGHTS

11

Writing the Complete Guide to anything is always going to be an audacious task, but for a subject as vast and diverse as weight training it was a serious challenge. Inevitably, there are limitations with any text on this vast subject, but I hope you will think that this book goes some way to doing this great subject justice and that it gives you renewed enthusiasm and inspiration for this fantastic pursuit.

I have done my best to put together a resource that will give you maximum possible value in terms of really applicable tools and hope that as you read it you will feel excited about trying out some of the exercises and programming techniques that are shown here. Of course, many training methods and programmes haven't made it into this book either through a lack of substantive evidence for their inclusion, or as is more likely the case a simple lack of space to include them all. I hope this inspires you to go out and research further to see what you can find.

Lastly, I have included some thoughts to leave you with that might help save you from some of the frustrations I experienced when starting to lift weights.

- Diet and Lifestyle can make or break your training programme. Getting your diet right and staying off the alcohol and junk is critical to getting the best from your weight training programme, whether you are looking to gain weight or lose it!

  Taking time to learn about decent nutrition is time well spent. Alcohol, for example, will send your testosterone levels plummeting, reducing your potential for muscle growth and serve only to increase your body fat levels. So, while you may focus on the one hour you spend *in* the gym, it's important to be aware of the 23 hours you spend out of it.

- Be careful what you copy. There are some fantastic authors on the internet, sharing valuable knowledge. But be careful what you copy. Taking a programme aimed for an elite athlete and applying it to the once-a-week over '70s' exercise class is not likely to get the results you want. All internet training programmes are examples of programmes that can work for someone at some point, but that doesn't necessarily make them right for you.

- There is **no** perfect training programme. You can spend hours searching for the 'ultimate fat burning' workout but it doesn't exist, so save your time by not bothering. Nothing works permanently and the perfect programme won't stay perfect. Each person reacts differently to training and has different needs and goals, find what works for you, not for someone else.

- Change nothing and nothing will change. Following on from my previous point, you need to keep things changing. As a rule you will be adapting to any given routine in as few as 6 exposures and some athletes will change their programme every workout to avoid stagnation. Aim to change your training approach every 4–6 weeks.

The more advanced and better trained you are, the more often you will need to do this.

- Keep workouts to an hour long. This is as much as for exercise adherence as anything else, but it will also prevent overtraining and adrenal exhaustion. Testosterone starts to decline seriously quickly over 45 minutes to an hour, so it's time to get that post-workout drink in and hit the showers after an hour. Those with more time, desire, and need should split their sessions into two a day, if necessary.

- Never sacrifice quality for quantity. As soon as you sacrifice the quality of your work for sheer quantity you might as well not bother. Make every rep and set you do of the highest quality. Concentrate on each one like it was the only one you are going to do in the whole workout and you will get far better results. Do not use cheating movements (such as using the lower back to swing the bar up on an arm curl) for the best part of the training. Instead, aim to perform movements with perfect form each time through the full range (unless performing specific movements such as partial range training or sports specific patterns that allow momentum).

- Ladies, *please* don't believe all you hear. If there is one giant section of the population who are subject to more misunderstanding about free weights, then it is women. Unfortunately, much of the women's media does little to assuage this, instead perpetuating the problems by what I call 'pink dumbbell syndrome' that implies women should only lift tiny weights (normally very slowly and for endless repetitions) to 'tone' the muscle or some such similar rubbish.

Women can achieve great benefits from using free weights and even more from including some higher intensity work into their training. Unfortunately, they are often denied this by a pathological fear of a lack of femininity and huge muscle growth. Believe me, were it really that simple to grow muscle every man and his dog would be in the gym.

However, I do realise that the weights area at the local gym is typically an intimidating environment and I believe that women-only weights rooms are an excellent idea. I am always disappointed to see that these rarely even contain a dumbbell over 5kg though. When health clubs wake up to women's needs in terms of weight training we may see a real improvement and increase in the amount of women lifting weights.

- Enjoy what you do. Weight training should be enjoyable. Sure, it is going to be hard graft at times and you will need to put effort in to get those results. However, going to the gym should not really be a chore that you do out of obligation more than anything else. The chances are if you feel like that then you won't be in the right frame of mind to get the results you are after. Not everyone needs to lift weights four or five times a week. Find an activity you really enjoy and then use weight training as a way of improving that activity and raising your performance at it. Weights can be beneficial to golfers, runners, cyclists, just about anyone, so try to balance it with the rest of your life to keep it all enjoyable.

Lastly, with the industry constantly changing and evolving it is good to keep an open mind to different approaches, while at the same time considering each on its merits and only applying it where appropriate. I encourage you to read more from other authors and sources and to try out different things for yourself, as there is always more than one way to go about it!

And on that little pearl of wisdom, I hope you enjoyed the book. It was a lot of work putting it together and I am constantly thankful to those strength coaches who have contributed to it through educating me and inspiring me to get better at what I do. I hope this book has the same effect on you.

Stay strong!
Graeme Marsh

BIBLIOGRAPHY

Baechle, T.R., Earle, R. *Essentials of Strength Training and Conditioning*, 2nd edition. Human Kinetics, Champaign IL. 2000.

Behm et al, 'Trunk muscle electromyographic activity with unstable and unilateral exercises', *Journal of Strength and Conditioning Research* 19(1):193–201. 2005.

Chaitow, L. *Muscle Energy Techniques,* 2nd edition. Churchill Livingstone Elsevier, London. 1999.

Fleck, S.J., Kraemer W.J. *Designing Resistance Training Programmes,* 3rd edition. Human Kinetics, Champaign IL. 2004.

Fleck, S.J., Kraemer, W.J. *Optimising Strength Training,* 1st edition. Human Kinetics, Champaign IL. 2007.

Kendall, F. *Muscles Testing and Function; With Posture and Pain,* 4th edition. Lippincott Williams & Wilkins, Philadephia PA. 1993.

Marsh, G.E. *Stronger and Fitter for Life,* 1st edition. A&C Black, London. 2007.

McGill. S. *Ultimate Back Fitness and Performance,* 3rd edition, Backfitpro Inc. Ontario. 2006.

Newton. H. *Explosive Lifting for Sports,* Human Kinetics, Champaign IL. 2006.

Poliquin, C. *Modern Trends in Strength Training,* 4th edition, Poliquin Performance Centres. 2006.

Poliquin, C. *Poliquin Principles: Successful methods for strength and mass development.* Poliquin Performance Centres. 2006.

Rippetoe, M. & Kilgore, L. *Practical Programming for Strength Training.* Aasgard Company, Texas. 2006.

Rippetoe, M. & Kilgore, L. *Starting Strength.* Aasgard Company, Texas. 2005.

Sahrmann, S. *Diagnosis and Treatment of Movement Impairment Syndromes.* Mosby, St Louis MI. 2002.

Schmidt, R.A., Wrisberg, C.A. *Motor Learning and Performance,* 2nd edition. Human Kinetics. Champaign IL. 2000.

Siff, M., *Supertraining,* 1st edition. Supertraining Institute, Denver. 1993.

Thibaudeau, C., *The Black Book of Training Secrets: Enhanced Edition.* F. Lepine. 2006.

Tippet, S.R., Voight, M.R., *Functional Progressions for Sports Rehabilitation,* Human Kinetics, Champaign IL. 1995.

Voight et al (eds), *Musculoskeletal Interventions.* McGraw-Hill. 2007.

Vossen et al. 'Comparison of Dynamic Push-Up Training and Plyometric Push-Up Training on Upper-Body Power and Strength. *The Journal of Strength and Conditioning Research* Vol. 14, No. 3, pp.248-253.

Zatsiorsky, V. *The Science and Practice of Strength Training.* Human Kinetics, Champaign IL. 1995.

GLOSSARY

Accommodation – The principle by which the response of the body to a set exercise or protocol reduces over time and use.

Adaptation – The process of change within the various systems of the body to a specific stimulus.

Aerobic activity – Any activity performed where energy production is dependant on the presence of oxygen. Often used incorrectly synonymously with 'cardio training'.

Anaerobic activity – Any activity performed where energy is generated without the presence of oxygen.

Anatomical Adaptation Phases – A phase of training where the intent is to stimulate anatomical or structural changes in body composition.

Barbell – A steel bar, typically chrome covered, that typically weighs 20kg and has weights secured by means of a collar on each end.

Basedowic or B-Overtraining – The classic type of overtraining that affects the sympathetic nervous system. Named after Basedow's Disease, which is associated with thyroid hyperactivity. Symptoms include fatigue, elevated pulse, increased sleep, soreness, stiffness, lack of motivation and unease.

Combination exercise – Any exercise that combines 2 or more recognised movements, such as a squat and press.

Compensatory Acceleration Training or CAT – The practice of deliberately aiming to accelerate the weight through the concentric part of the exercise to increase levels of muscular tension.

Complex exercise – Interchangeable term used to describe a sequence of exercises performed without rest. Typically performed with a barbell but also can be done with kettlebells or dumbbells.

Concentric action – A muscle action where the muscle shortens in length.

Concurrent training – The training of multiple outcomes over the same training day, week, or month with the intention to develop multi-faceted improvement of several systems.

Contralateral – The opposite side of the body.

Deadlift – An exercise where the weight is lifted from the 'dead' position on the floor.

Density – A function of work in relation to time. Workouts that involve high volumes of work with minimal rest are more 'dense'.

DOMS – Delayed Onset Muscle Soreness, a specific type of muscle soreness that occurs from 24–72 hours post-training.

Dumbbell – Hand held weight, can be round, hex, or Olympic and in a range of materials though rubber and chrome are most common.

Eccentric action – Muscle action where the muscle is lengthened under tension.

Eccentric training – A form of training using weights that cannot be lifted concentrically and instead are lowered and raised with assistance, or by employing a system such as weight releasers.

EPOC – Excess Post-Exercise Oxygen Consumption – referring to the increase in oxygen consumption seen post-training to replace depleted energy stores.

Farmers' walks – Traditional strongman exercise where a set distance is covered while carrying two large objects.

Fast twitch muscle – Muscle that has a higher activation threshold and is recruited during maximal efforts. Principle muscle responsible for speed and power.

General adaptation syndrome (GAS) – Model proposed by Hans Selye to explain the response of the body to a stressor.

Growth Hormone – Anabolic hormone secreted by the pituitary gland, implicated in fat reduction and stimulated through strenuous exercise such as weight lifting.

Hybrid exercise – An exercise that combines together two or more conventional movements, similar to a combination exercise.

Hybrid repetition – A sequence of exercises performed together to make one repetition.

Hypertrophy – The scientific term for increasing muscle cross-sectional area.

Individualisation – The principle that dictates the need for individualised training programme design and implementation.

Intensity – A measure of the percentage of the trainee's 1 repetition maximum.

Intra-abdominal pressure or IAP – The increase in abdominal pressure that is created to support the spine during lifting tasks.

Ipsilateral – Same side of the body.

Isometric action – A muscle action where there is no visible change in muscle length and hence no change in joint angle.

Isometric training – The use of isometric muscle actions to generate hypertrophy and maximal muscle activation.

Kettlebell – Russian inspired training tool with a wider handle and different weight position to a dumbbell.

Kinetic chain – A term used to refer to the links between the various connective tissues of the body, including muscle and fascia.

Lactate – A by-product of anaerobic energy metabolism that can be used by skeletal and heart muscle for energy.

Lordotic/Lordosis – The inward facing curve of the lumbar spine. Someone who is lordotic is said to have an overly pronounced curve.

Maximal strength/training – Employing methods of training specifically intended to increase maximal strength.

Maximal velocity – Moving an object at the highest speed possible.

Maximals – Sometimes also called 'Singles' refers to lifting a weight once only.

Medicine ball – Weighted leather or fabric bound ball.

Mesocycle – Science term for a training cycle of typically 4–6 weeks.

Neural mechanisms – The various aspects of the nervous system that are responsible for increases in strength.

NSAID – Non-steroidal Anti-Inflammatory

Overload – Training principle which dictates the need for sufficient amount of overload in order to stimulate a training adaptation.

Overtraining – Condition of nervous system or endocrine system fatigue resulting in sub-standard performance.

Parasympathetic nervous system – The branch of the autonomic nervous system responsible for a range of functions such as digestion, slowing heart rate and respiration.

Periodisation – Term used to describe the process of altering training variables over time to elicit a specific training adaptation.

Peripheral heart action (PHA) techniques – Method of training that supersets upper and lower body exercises, using whole body free weight movements. Well suited to fat reduction training methods.

Plateau – A period of being stuck lifting a certain weight without progress.

Plyometrics – A specialised training method that is typified by a rapid pre-stretching of the muscles before an explosive concentric effort.

PNF – Proprioceptive Neuromuscular Facilitation, a system first developed for treating stroke victims that has a set of principles and is characterised by the use of spiral diagonal movement patterns.

Post-Tetanic Potentiation or PTP – The resonant after-effect of a maximal or near-maximal muscle contraction that can facilitate greater voluntary muscle activation subsequently.

Powerbag – Training tool based on the sandbag, particularly useful for explosive 'release' training.

Prehabilitation – Modern term used to describe the process of selecting training methods aimed specifically at reducing the likelihood of injury.

Pronated – Can refer to the 'rolling inwards' of the foot, flattening the arch. Also refers to the rotation downwards of the forearm so the palm faces the floor.

Proprioception – The feedback system of the body that enables us to balance, move, function, and detect forces and positions of our muscles and joints.

RM – Repetition Maximum

Sequenced training – Where training variables are training sequentially in phases with each phase building on the adaptations from the previous one.

Slow twitch muscle – Smaller, low threshold muscle fibres more suited to aerobic work over longer time periods.

Specificity – The principle that dictates that any adaptation in the body will be specific to the demands that created that adaptation.

Split routine – The use of a training programme that divides the body into various parts or movements to enable more intensive work on one aspect during the workout.

Spotter – Person who ensures the safety of the lifter during heavy efforts.

Stability balls – Inflatable ball that originated in physical therapy and is commonly used to create an unstable surface to work from.

Steady-state session – Training method also called 'Steady-Rate' when energy is produced aerobically and the demand for it does not exceed this system's capacity.

Sticking point – The point in a lift at which a lifter will typically fail, usually the biomechanically weakest point in the lift.

Strength deficit – The difference between absolute (involuntary) strength and a maximally produced voluntary effort.

Stretch reflex – The protective reflex action of muscle spindles during the lengthening of a muscle, resulting in a concentric contraction. Can also be harnessed deliberately to generate elastic energy.

Sub-maximal strength – The use of loads that are below that of the trainee's 1RM.

Supinated – A rolling of the foot outwards or rotating the palm of the hand upwards.

Supramaximal training – The use of loads well above the concentric maximum to stimulate maximal levels of muscle activation and recruitment.

Testosterone – A key anabolic hormone and androgen.

Triple extension – The combined extension that occurs in the ankle, knee, and hip during explosive lifts such as the clean or snatch.

TRX system – A bodyweight oriented training device that anchors to a point above the training and utilises handles attached to two webbing straps.

Undulating (non-linear) periodisation – A system of periodisation characterised by frequent changes in a range of training variables.

Valsalva maneuver – Holding a breath forced against the closed airway to generate high levels of intra-abdominal pressure.

VO2 – The unit of measure of oxygen consumption.

Wave loading – A repetition system that can be used for a range of training outcomes, although typically used in relative strength training.

INDEX

Page numbers with g are glossary terms. Page numbers in italics show illustrations.

NOTES

ALSO AVAILABLE

The Complete Guide to Strength Training – 4th Edition

Anita Bean

This bestselling book is essential reading for anyone wanting to increase strength and resculpt their body. Following the principles of strength training and muscle growth, Anita Bean – a former British Natural Bodybuilding Champion – shows you how to achieve your goals with step-by-step guides to over 100 exercises and programmes for beginner, intermediate and advanced levels. Now updated in full-colour, this book is the definitive strength training handbook.

Available from all good bookshops or online. For more details on these and other A&C Black sport and fitness titles, please go to www.acblack.com.